D1443585

ENGINEERING

THIRD EDITION

Ferguson
An imprint of Infobase Publishing

Careers in Focus: Engineering, Third Edition

Copyright © 2007 by Infobase Publishing

Ferguson
An imprint of Infobase Publishing
132 West 31st Street
New York NY 10001

Library of Congress Cataloging-in-Publication Data

Careers in focus. Engineering.—3rd ed.
    p. cm.
Includes index.
ISBN-13: 978-0-8160-6571-4
ISBN-10: 0-8160-6571-3
    1. Engineering—Vocational guidance—Juvenile literature. 2. Vocational guidance—Juvenile literature. I. J.G. Ferguson Publishing Company. II. Title: Engineering.
    TA157.C283 2007
    620.0023—dc22

Ferguson books are available at special discounts when purchased in bulk quantities for businesses, associations, institutions, or sales promotions. Please call our Special Sales Department in New York at (212) 967-8800 or (800) 322-8755.

You can find Ferguson on the World Wide Web at http://www.fergpubco.com

Text design by David Strelecky
Cover design by Salvatore Luongo

Printed in the United States of America

MP MSRF 10 9 8 7 6 5 4 3 2 1

This book is printed on acid-free paper.

Table of Contents

Introduction 1
Aerospace Engineers 5
Biomedical Engineers 16
Chemical Engineers 23
Civil Engineers 35
Electrical and Electronics Engineers 43
Engineering Technicians 59
Environmental Engineers 69
Hardware Engineers 78
Industrial Engineers 89
Materials Engineers 97
Mechanical Engineers 108
Mining Engineers 117
Nuclear Engineers 127
Optical Engineers 136
Packaging Engineers 145
Petroleum Engineers 156
Quality Control Engineers 166
Robotics Engineers 174
Software Engineers 183
Transportation Engineers 191
Index 197

Introduction

The work of engineers has a more widespread impact on people than just about any other discipline. Engineers have influenced discoveries and inventions that are part of our everyday lives more than any other professionals. They use scientific knowledge and tools to design products, structures, and machines. Most engineers specialize in a particular area but have a base of knowledge and training that can be applied in many fields. Electrical and electronics engineers, for example, work in the medical, computer, missile guidance, and power distribution fields. A young person embarking on a career as an engineer has a tremendous range of choices regarding the type of work he or she wants to pursue.

A nuclear power station provides a good example of how different engineering specialties work together. The contributions of civil engineers include helping select the site for the power station and developing blueprints for all structural details of the reactor building. Nuclear engineers handle every stage of the production of nuclear energy, from the processing of nuclear fuels to the disposal of radioactive wastes. Environmental engineers also find ways to safely dispose of such wastes. Mechanical engineers develop and build engines that produce power using the nuclear fuel. Electrical engineers design equipment to distribute the electricity to thousands of customers over a wide area. Even an engineering discipline that may seem unrelated to nuclear power, biomedical engineering, is essential for the people who will be employed at the plant. The device workers wear to detect the levels of radiation their bodies absorb over a period of time was developed by biomedical engineers.

All engineers engage in one of five areas of work: research, development, application, management, and maintenance. Engineers who work in research are responsible for investigating new materials, processes, or principles for practical applications of ideas and materials. Engineers who work in development use the research results to determine how best to apply them to their practical functions. Application engineers produce the actual materials, machines, and methods designed by research and development engineers. Management and maintenance engineers keep the developed idea working and make improvements and adjustments.

Engineers have traditionally enjoyed great employment security and good pay and benefits because their work is so essential to maintaining and advancing America's infrastructure and industry.

Even in times of economic decline, engineers' jobs are generally safe. Demand will continue to be strong for engineers with a solid math and science background and training in new technologies.

Each article in *Careers in Focus: Engineering* discusses a particular engineering-related career in detail. The articles appear in Ferguson's *Encyclopedia of Careers and Vocational Guidance,* but have been updated and revised with the latest information from the U.S. Department of Labor, professional organizations, and other sources. The following paragraphs detail the sections and features that appear in the book.

The **Quick Facts** section provides a brief summary of the career, including recommended school subjects, personal skills, work environment, minimum educational requirements, salary ranges, certification or licensing requirements, and employment outlook. This section also provides acronyms and identification numbers for the following government classification indexes: the Dictionary of Occupational Titles (DOT), the Guide to Occupational Exploration (GOE), the National Occupational Classification (NOC) Index, and the Occupational Information Network (O*NET)-Standard Occupational Classification System (SOC) index. The DOT, GOE, and O*NET-SOC indexes have been created by the U.S. government; the NOC index is Canada's career classification system. Readers can use the identification numbers listed in the Quick Facts section to access further information about a career. Print editions of the DOT (*Dictionary of Occupational Titles.* Indianapolis, Ind.: JIST Works, 1991) and GOE (*The Complete Guide for Occupational Exploration.* Indianapolis, Ind.: JIST Works, 1993) are available at libraries. Electronic versions of the NOC (http://www23.hrdc-drhc.gc.ca) and O*NET-SOC (http://online.onetcenter.org) are available on the Internet. When no DOT, GOE, NOC, or O*NET-SOC numbers are present, this means that the U.S. Department of Labor or Human Resources Development Canada have not created a numerical designation for this career. In this instance, you will see the acronym "N/A," or not available.

The **Overview** section is a brief introductory description of the duties and responsibilities involved in this career. Oftentimes, a career may have a variety of job titles. When this is the case, alternative career titles are presented. The **History** section describes the history of the particular job as it relates to the overall development of its industry or field. **The Job** describes the primary and secondary duties of the job. **Requirements** discusses high school and postsecondary education and training requirements, any certification or licensing that is necessary, and other personal requirements for success in the job. **Exploring** offers suggestions on how to gain experience in or knowledge of the particular job before making a firm educational and financial commitment. The focus is on what can be done while still in high school (or in the early years of college) to gain a better understanding of the job. The **Employers** section gives an overview of typical places of employment for the job. **Starting Out** discusses the best ways to land that first job, be it through the college placement office, newspaper ads, or personal contact. The **Advancement** section describes what kind of career path to expect from the job and how to get there. **Earnings** lists salary ranges and describes the typical fringe benefits. The **Work Environment** section describes the typical surroundings and conditions of employment—whether indoors or outdoors, noisy or quiet, social or independent. Also discussed are typical hours worked, any seasonal fluctuations, and the stresses and strains of the job. The **Outlook** section summarizes the job in terms of the general economy and industry projections. For the most part, Outlook information is obtained from the U.S. Bureau of Labor Statistics and is supplemented by information taken from professional associations. Job growth terms follow those used in the *Occupational Outlook Handbook.* Growth described as "much faster than the average" means an increase of 27 percent or more. Growth described as "faster than the average" means an increase of 18 to 26 percent. Growth described as "about as fast as the average" means an increase of 9 to 17 percent. Growth described as "more slowly than the average" means an increase of 0 to 8 percent. "Decline" means a decrease by any amount. Each article ends with **For More Information,** which lists organizations that provide information on training, education, internships, scholarships, and job placement.

Careers in Focus: Engineering also includes photographs, informative sidebars, and interviews with professionals in the field.

Aerospace Engineers

OVERVIEW

Aerospace engineering encompasses the fields of aeronautical (aircraft) and astronautical (spacecraft) engineering. *Aerospace engineers* work in teams to design, build, and test machines that fly within the earth's atmosphere and beyond. Although aerospace science is a very specialized discipline, it is also considered one of the most diverse. This field of engineering draws from such subjects as physics, mathematics, earth science, aerodynamics, and biology. Some aerospace engineers specialize in designing one complete machine, perhaps a commercial aircraft, whereas others focus on separate components such as for missile guidance systems. There are approximately 76,000 aerospace engineers working in the United States.

HISTORY

The roots of aerospace engineering can be traced as far back as when people first dreamed of being able to fly. Thousands of years ago, the Chinese developed kites and later experimented with gunpowder as a source of propulsion. In the 15th century, Renaissance artist Leonardo da Vinci created drawings of two devices that were designed to fly. One, the ornithopter, was supposed to fly the way birds do, by flapping its wings; the other was designed as a rotating screw, closer in form to today's helicopter.

In 1783, Joseph and Jacques Montgolfier of France designed the first hot-air balloon that could be used for manned flight. In 1799, an English baron, Sir George Cayley, designed an aircraft that was one of the first not to be considered "lighter than air," as balloons were. He developed a fixed-wing structure that led to his creation of the first glider in 1849. Much experimentation was performed in gliders and the science of aerodynamics through the late 1800s. In 1903, the first mechanically powered and controlled flight was completed in a craft designed by Orville and Wilbur Wright. The big boost in airplane development occurred during World War I. In the early years of the war, aeronautical engineering encompassed a variety of engineering skills applied toward the development of flying machines. Civil engineering principles were used in structural design, while early airplane engines were devised by automobile engineers. Aerodynamic design itself was primarily empirical, with many answers coming from liquid flow concepts established in marine engineering.

The evolution of the airplane continued during both world wars, with steady technological developments in materials science, propulsion, avionics, and stability and control. Airplanes became larger and faster. Airplanes are commonplace today, but commercial flight became a frequent mode of transportation only as recently as the 1960s and 1970s.

Robert Goddard developed and flew the first liquid-propelled rocket in 1926. The technology behind liquid propulsion continued to evolve, and the first U.S. liquid rocket engine was tested in 1938. More sophisticated rockets were eventually created to enable aircraft to be launched into space. The world's first artificial satellite, *Sputnik I,* was launched by the Soviets in 1957. In 1961, President John F. Kennedy urged the United States to be the first country to put a man on the moon; on July 20, 1969, astronauts Neil Armstrong and Edwin Aldrin Jr. accomplished that goal.

Today, aerospace engineers design spacecraft that explore beyond the earth's atmosphere, such as space shuttles and rockets. They create missiles and military aircraft of many types, such as fighters, bombers, observers, and transports. Today's engineers go beyond the dreams of merely learning to fly. For example, in 1998, the United States and 15 other countries began a series of joint missions into space to assemble a planned International Space Station. On the ground, space professionals, including aerospace engineers, have played a vital role in developing equipment that is used on the station.

THE JOB

Although the creation of aircraft and spacecraft involve professionals from many branches of engineering (e.g., materials, electrical, and mechanical), aerospace engineers in particular are responsible for the total design of the craft, including its shape, performance, propulsion, and guidance control system. In the field of aerospace engineering, professional responsibilities vary widely depending on the specific job description. *Aeronautical engineers* work specifically with aircraft systems, and *astronautical engineers* specialize in spacecraft systems.

Throughout their education and training, aerospace engineers thoroughly learn the complexities involved in how materials and structures perform under tremendous stress. In general, they are called upon to apply their knowledge of the following subjects: propulsion, aerodynamics, thermodynamics, fluid mechanics, flight mechanics, and structural analysis. Less technically scientific issues must also often be dealt with, such as cost analysis, reliability studies, maintainability, operations research, marketing, and management.

There are many professional titles given to certain aerospace engineers. *Analytical engineers* use engineering and mathematical theory to solve questions that arise during the design phase. *Stress analysts* determine how the weight and loads of structures behave under a variety of conditions. This analysis is performed with computers and complex formulas.

Computational fluid dynamic (CFD) engineers use sophisticated high-speed computers to develop models used in the study of fluid dynamics. Using simulated systems, they determine how elements flow around objects; simulation saves time and money and eliminates risks involved with actual testing. As computers become more complex, so do the tasks of the CFD engineer.

Design aerospace engineers draw from the expertise of many other specialists. They devise the overall structure of components and entire crafts, meeting the specifications developed by those more specialized in aerodynamics, astrodynamics, and structural engineering. Design engineers use computer-aided design programs for many of their tasks.

Manufacturing aerospace engineers develop the plans for producing the complex components that make up aircraft and spacecraft. They work with the designers to ensure that the plans are economically feasible and will produce efficient, effective components.

Materials aerospace engineers determine the suitability of the various materials that are used to produce aerospace vehicles. Aircraft and spacecraft require the appropriate tensile strength, density, and rigidity for the particular environments they are subjected to. Determining how materials such as steel, glass, and even chemical compounds react to temperature and stress is an important part of the materials engineer's responsibilities.

Quality control is a task that aerospace engineers perform throughout the development, design, and manufacturing processes. The finished product must be evaluated for its reliability, vulnerability, and how it is to be maintained and supported.

Marketing and sales aerospace engineers work with customers, usually industrial corporations and the government, informing them of product performance. They act as a liaison between the technical engineers and the clients to help ensure that the products delivered are performing as planned. Sales engineers also need to anticipate the needs of the customer, as far ahead as possible, to inform their companies of potential marketing opportunities. They also keep abreast of their competitors and need to understand how to structure contracts effectively.

REQUIREMENTS

High School

While in high school, follow a college preparatory program. Doing well in mathematics and science classes is vital if you want to pursue a career in any type of engineering field. The American Society for Engineering Education advises students to take calculus and trigonometry in high school, as well as laboratory science classes. Such courses provide the skills you'll need for problem solving, an essential skill in any type of engineering.

Postsecondary Training

Aerospace engineers need a bachelor's degree to enter the field. More advanced degrees are necessary for those interested in teaching or research and development positions.

While a major in aerospace engineering is the norm, other majors are acceptable. For example, the National Aeronautics and Space Administration recommends a degree in any of a variety of disciplines, including biomedical engineering, ceramics engineering, chemistry, industrial engineering, materials science, metallurgy, optical engineering, and oceanography. You should make sure the college you choose has an accredited engineering program. The Accreditation Board for Engineering and Technology (ABET) sets minimum education standards for programs in these fields. Graduation from an ABET-accredited school is a requirement for becoming licensed in many states, so it is important to select an accredited school. Currently, approximately 360 colleges and universities offer ABET-accredited bachelor's of engineering programs. Visit ABET's Web site (http://www.abet.org) for a listing of accredited schools.

Some aerospace engineers complete master's degrees and even doctoral work before entering this field. Advanced degrees can significantly increase an engineer's earnings. Students continuing on to graduate school will study research and development, with a thesis required for a master's degree and a dissertation for a doctorate.

Certification or Licensing

Most states require engineers to be licensed. There are two levels of licensing for engineers. Professional Engineers (PEs) have graduated from an accredited engineering curriculum, have four years of engineering experience, and have passed a written exam. Engineering graduates need not wait until they have four years experience, however, to start the licensure process. Those who pass the Fundamentals of Engineering examination after graduating are called Engineers-in-Training (EITs) or Engineer Interns (EIs). The EIT certification usually is valid for 10 years. After acquiring suitable work experience, EITs can take the second examination, the Principles and Practice of Engineering exam, to gain full PE licensure. For more information on licensing and examination requirements, visit http://www.ncees.org.

In order to ensure that aerospace engineers are kept up to date on their quickly changing field, many states have imposed continuing education requirements for relicensure.

Other Requirements

Aerospace engineers should enjoy completing detailed work, problem solving, and participating in group efforts. Mathematical, science, and computer skills are a must. Equally important, however, are the abilities to communicate ideas, share in teamwork, and visualize the forms and functions of structures. Curiosity, inventiveness, and the willingness to continue learning from experiences are excellent qualities to have for this type of work.

EXPLORING

If you like to work on model airplanes and rockets, you may be a good candidate for an aerospace engineering career. Consider working on special research assignments supervised by your science and math teachers for helpful experience. You may also want to try working on cars and boats, which provides a good opportunity to discover more about aerodynamics. A part-time job with a local manufacturer can give you some exposure to product engineering and development.

Books to Read

Anderson, John David, Jr. *The Airplane: A History of Its Technology*. Reston, Va.: American Institute of Aeronautics and Astronautics, 2002.

Anderson, John David, Jr. *A History of Aerodynamics: And Its Impact on Flying Machines*. New York: Cambridge University Press, 1997.

Chiles, James R. *Inviting Disaster: Lessons from the Edge of Technology*. New York: HarperBusiness, 2002.

Maples, Wallace. *Opportunities in Aerospace Careers*. 3d ed. New York: McGraw-Hill, 2002.

Rinard, Judith, and Smithsonian National Air and Space Museum. *The Story of Flight*. Richmond Hill, ON, Canada; Firefly Books, 2002.

Exciting opportunities are often available at summer camps and academic programs throughout the country. For instance, the University of North Dakota (see address listed at the end of this article) presents an aerospace camp focusing on study and career exploration that includes instruction in model rocketry and flight. However, admission to the camp is competitive; the camp usually consists of two 10-day programs for 32 students each.

It is also a good idea to join a science club while in high school. For example, the Junior Engineering Technical Society provides members with opportunities to enter academic competitions, explore career opportunities, and design model structures. Contact information is available at the end of this article.

Aerospace America (http://www.aiaa.org/aerospace), published by the American Institute of Aeronautics and Astronautics, is a helpful magazine for exploring careers in aerospace. You should also check out the American Society for Engineering Education's precollege Web site, http://www.engineeringk12.org/students/default.htm, for general information about careers in engineering, as well as answers to frequently asked questions about engineering. In addition, the society offers *Engineering, Go For It*!, a comprehensive brochure about careers. It is available for a small fee.

EMPLOYERS

The U.S. Department of Labor reports that approximately 76,000 aerospace engineers are employed in the United States. Many aircraft-related engineering jobs are found in Alabama, California, and Florida, where large aerospace companies are located. Nearly 60 percent of all aerospace engineers work in product and parts manufacturing. Government agencies, such as the Department of Defense and the National Aeronautics and Space Administration, employ approximately 12 percent of aerospace engineers. Other employers include engineering services, research and testing services, and electronics manufacturers.

STARTING OUT

Many students begin their careers while completing their studies through work-study arrangements that sometimes turn into full-time jobs. Most aerospace manufacturers actively recruit engineering students, conducting on-campus interviews and other activities to locate the best candidates. Students preparing to graduate can also send out resumes to companies active in the aerospace industry and arrange interviews. Many colleges and universities also staff career services centers, which are often good places to find leads for new job openings.

Students can also apply directly to agencies of the federal government concerned with aerospace development and implementation. Applications can be made through the Office of Personnel Management or through an agency's own hiring department.

Professional associations, such as the National Society of Professional Engineers and the American Institute of Aeronautics and Astronautics, offer job placement services, including career advice, job listings, and training. Their contact information is listed at the end of this article.

ADVANCEMENT

As in most engineering fields, there tends to be a hierarchy of workers in the various divisions of aerospace engineering. This is true in research, design and development, production, and teaching. In an entry-level job, one is considered simply an engineer, perhaps a junior engineer. After a certain amount of experience is gained, depending on the position, one moves on to work as a project engineer, supervising others. Then, as a managing engineer, one has further responsibilities over a number of project engineers and their teams. At the top of the hierarchy is the position of *chief engineer,* which involves authority over managing engineers and additional decision-making responsibilities.

As engineers move up the career ladder, the type of responsibilities they have tend to change. Junior engineers are highly involved in technical matters and scientific problem solving. As managers and chiefs, engineers have the responsibilities of supervising, cost analyzing, and relating with clients.

All engineers must continue to learn and study technological progress throughout their careers. It is important to keep abreast of engineering advancements and trends by reading industry journals and taking courses. Such courses are offered by professional associations or colleges. In aerospace engineering especially, changes occur rapidly, and those who seek promotions must be prepared. Those who are employed by colleges and universities must continue teaching and conducting research if they want to have tenured (more guaranteed) faculty positions.

EARNINGS

In 2005, the median salary for aerospace engineers was $84,090 per year, according to the U.S. Department of Labor. Experienced engineers employed by the federal government tended to earn more, with a mean salary of $93,050. Federal employees also enjoy greater job security and often more generous vacation and retirement benefits. The most experienced aerospace engineers earned salaries of more than $117,680 annually.

Aerospace engineers with bachelor's degrees earned average starting salaries of $50,993 per year, according to a 2005 salary survey conducted by the National Association of Colleges and Employers. With a master's degree, candidates were offered $62,930, and with a Ph.D., $72,529.

All engineers can expect to receive vacation and sick pay, paid holidays, health insurance, life insurance, and retirement programs.

WORK ENVIRONMENT

Aerospace engineers work in various settings depending on their job description. Those involved in research and design usually work in a traditional office setting. They spend considerable time at computers and drawing boards. Engineers involved with the testing of components and structures often work outside at test sites or in laboratories where controlled testing conditions can be created.

In the manufacturing area of the aerospace industry, engineers often work on the factory floor itself, assembling components and making sure that they conform to design specifications. This job requires much walking around large production facilities, such as aircraft factories or spacecraft assembly plants.

Engineers are sometimes required to travel to other locations to consult with companies that make materials and other needed components. Others travel to remote test sites to observe and participate in flight testing.

Aerospace engineers are also employed by the Federal Aviation Administration and commercial airline companies. These engineers perform a variety of duties, including performance analysis and crash investigations. Companies that are involved with satellite communications need the expertise of aerospace engineers to better interpret the many aspects of the space environment and the problems involved with getting a satellite launched into space.

OUTLOOK

Employment in this field is expected to grow more slowly than the average for all occupations through 2014, according to the U.S. Department of Labor. Shrinking space program budgets, increased job efficiency, and the continuing wave of corporate downsizing have all combined to cut severely into the aerospace industry.

Nevertheless, the aerospace industry remains vital to the health of the national economy. Increasing airline traffic and the need to replace aging airplanes with quieter and more fuel-efficient aircraft will boost demand for aerospace engineers over the next decade. The federal government has increased defense budgets in order to build up the armed forces. More aerospace engineers will be needed to repair and add to the current air fleet, as well as to improve defense technology. Engineers are also needed to help make commercial aircraft safer, designing and installing reinforced cockpit doors and onboard security screening equipment to protect pilots, crew, and commercial passengers.

Despite cutbacks in the space program, the development of new space technology and increasing commercial uses for that technology will continue to require qualified engineers. Facing reduced demand in the United States, aerospace companies are increasing their sales overseas, and depending on the world economy and foreign demand, this new market could create a demand for new workers in the industry.

The U.S. Department of Labor reports that the number of students graduating with degrees in aerospace engineering has declined in recent years, and graduates will be needed to fill new positions, as well as those vacated by engineers who retire or leave the field for other careers.

FOR MORE INFORMATION

For a list of accredited schools and colleges, contact
Accreditation Board for Engineering and Technology Inc.
111 Market Place, Suite 1050
Baltimore, MD 21202-7116
Tel: 410-347-7700
http://www.abet.org

Contact AIA for publications with information on aerospace technologies, careers, and space.
Aerospace Industries Association of America (AIA)
1000 Wilson Boulevard, Suite 1700
Arlington, VA 22209-3928
Tel: 703-358-1000
http://www.aia-aerospace.org

For information about scholarships, colleges, and career opportunities, contact the following organizations:
American Institute of Aeronautics and Astronautics
1801 Alexander Bell Drive, Suite 500
Reston, VA 20191-4344
Tel: 800-639-2422
http://www.aiaa.org

American Society for Engineering Education
1818 N Street, NW, Suite 600
Washington, DC 20036-2479
Tel: 202-331-3500
http://www.asee.org

The following organization offers information geared specifically toward students.
Junior Engineering Technical Society
1420 King Street, Suite 405
Alexandria, VA 22314-2794
Tel: 703-548-5387
Email: info@jets.org
http://www.jets.org

For career and licensing information, contact
National Society of Professional Engineers
1420 King Street

Alexandria, VA 22314-2794
Tel: 703-684-2800
http://www.nspe.org/students

For information on aerospace programs and summer camps, contact
University of North Dakota
John D. Odegard School of Aerospace Sciences
Clifford Hall, Room 512
4149 University Avenue, Stop 9008
Grand Forks, ND 58202-9008
Tel: 800-258-1525
http://www.aero.und.edu

Biomedical Engineers

QUICK FACTS

School Subjects
Biology
Chemistry

Personal Skills
Helping/teaching
Technical/scientific

Work Environment
Primarily indoors
Primarily one location

Minimum Education Level
Bachelor's degree

Salary Range
$44,060 to $71,840 to
$113,590+

Certification or Licensing
Voluntary

Outlook
Much faster than the average

DOT
019

GOE
02.02.01

NOC
2148

O*NET-SOC
17-2031.00

OVERVIEW

Biomedical engineers are highly trained scientists who use engineering and life science principles to research biological aspects of animal and human life. They develop new theories, and they modify, test, and prove existing theories on life systems. They design health care instruments and devices or apply engineering principles to the study of human systems. There are approximately 9,700 biomedical engineers employed in the United States.

HISTORY

Biomedical engineering is one of many new professions created by advancements in technology. It is an interdisciplinary field that brings together two respected professions: biology and engineering.

Biology, of course, is the study of life, and engineering, in broad terms, studies sources of energy in nature and the properties of matter in a way that is useful to humans, particularly in machines, products, and structures. A combination of the two fields, biomedical engineering, developed primarily after 1945 as new technology allowed for the application of engineering principles to biology. The artificial heart is just one in a long list of the products of biomedical engineering. Other products include artificial organs, prosthetics, the use of lasers in surgery, cryosurgery, and ultrasonics, and the use of computers and thermography in diagnosis.

THE JOB

Using engineering principles to solve medical and health-related problems, the biomedical engineer works closely with life scientists,

A biomedical engineer at work in a laboratory. *(Agricultural Research Service)*

members of the medical profession, and chemists. Most of the work revolves around the laboratory. There are three interrelated work areas: research, design, and teaching.

Biomedical research is multifaceted and broad in scope. It calls upon engineers to apply their knowledge of mechanical, chemical, and electrical engineering as well as anatomy and physiology in the study of living systems. Using computers, biomedical engineers use their knowledge of graphic and related technologies to develop mathematical models that simulate physiological systems.

In biomedical engineering design, medical instruments and devices are developed. Engineers work on artificial organs, ultrasonic imagery devices, cardiac pacemakers, and surgical lasers, for example. They design and build systems that will update hospital, laboratory, and clinical procedures. They also train health care personnel in the proper use of this new equipment.

Biomedical engineering is taught on the university level. Teachers conduct classes, advise students, serve on academic committees, and supervise or conduct research.

Within biomedical engineering, an individual may concentrate on a particular specialty area. Some of the well-established specialties are *bioinstrumentation, biomechanics, biomaterials, systems physiology, clinical engineering,* and *rehabilitation engineering.* These specialty areas frequently depend on one another.

Biomechanics is mechanics applied to biological or medical problems. Examples include the artificial heart, the artificial kidney, and the artificial hip. *Biomaterials* is the study of the optimal materials with which to construct such devices, *bioinstrumentation* is the science of measuring physiological functions. *Systems physiology* uses engineering strategies, techniques, and tools to gain a comprehensive and integrated understanding of living organisms ranging from bacteria to humans. Biomedical engineers in this specialty examine such things as the biochemistry of metabolism and the control of limb movements.

Rehabilitation engineering is a new and growing specialty area of biomedical engineering. Its goal is to expand the capabilities and improve the quality of life for individuals with physical impairments. Rehabilitation engineers often work directly with the disabled person and modify equipment for individual use.

REQUIREMENTS

High School
You can best prepare for a career as a biomedical engineer by taking courses in biology, chemistry, physics, mathematics, drafting, and computers. Communication and problem-solving skills are necessary, so classes in English, writing, and logic are important. Participating in science clubs and competing in science fairs will give you the opportunity to design and invent systems and products.

Postsecondary Training

Most biomedical engineers have an undergraduate degree in biomedical engineering or a related field and a master's degree in some facet of biomedical engineering. Undergraduate study is roughly divided into halves. The first two years are devoted to theoretical subjects, such as abstract physics and differential equations in addition to the core curriculum most undergraduates take. The third and fourth years include more applied science. Worldwide, there are over 80 colleges and universities that offer programs in biomedical engineering.

During graduate programs, students work on research or product development projects headed by faculty.

Certification or Licensing

Engineers whose work may affect the life, health, or safety of the public must be registered according to regulations in all 50 states and the District of Columbia. Applicants for registration must have received a degree from an American Board for Engineering and Technology-accredited engineering program and have four years of experience. They must also pass a written examination administered by the state in which they wish to work.

Other Requirements

You should have a strong commitment to learning if you plan on becoming a biomedical engineer. You should be scientifically inclined and be able to apply that knowledge in problem solving. Becoming a biomedical engineer requires long years of schooling because a biomedical engineer needs to be an expert in the fields of engineering and biology. Also, biomedical engineers have to be familiar with chemical, material, and electrical engineering as well as physiology and computers.

EXPLORING

Undergraduate courses offer a great deal of exposure to the field. Working in a hospital where biomedical engineers are employed can also provide you with insight into the field, as can interviews with practicing or retired biomedical engineers.

EMPLOYERS

There are approximately 9,700 biomedical engineers working in the United States. More than 34 percent are employed in scientific research and development services and pharmaceutical and medicine manufacturing. In addition, many biomedical engineers are employed in hospitals and medical institutions, for companies that produce medical supplies and instruments, and in research and educational facilities. Employment opportunities also exist in government regulatory agencies.

STARTING OUT

A variety of routes may be taken to gain employment as a biomedical engineer. Recent graduates may use college placement services, or they may apply directly to employers, often to personnel offices in hospitals and industry. A job may be secured by answering an advertisement in the employment section of a newspaper. Information on job openings is also available at the local office of the U.S. Employment Service.

ADVANCEMENT

Advancement opportunities are tied directly to educational and research background. In a nonteaching capacity, a biomedical engineer with an advanced degree can rise to a supervisory position. In teaching, a doctorate is usually necessary to become a full professor. By demonstrating excellence in research, teaching, and departmental committee involvement, one can move from instructor to assistant professor and then to full professor, department chair, or even dean.

Qualifying for and receiving research grant funding can also be a means of advancing one's career in both the nonteaching and teaching sectors.

EARNINGS

The amount a biomedical engineer earns is dependent upon education, experience, and type of employer. According to the U.S. Department of Labor, biomedical engineers had a median yearly income of $71,840 in 2005. At the low end of the pay scale, 10 percent earned less than $44,060 per year, and at the high end, 10 percent earned more than $113,590 annually.

According to a 2005 survey by the National Association of Colleges and Employers, the average beginning salary for those with bachelor's degrees in bioengineering/biomedical sciences was $48,503.

The American Association of University Professors reports that assistant professors who teach in the top paying disciplines (which includes health professions and engineering) earned an average of $58,5766 for 2003. Those who were full professors earned an average of $100,682 during that same period.

Biomedical engineers can expect benefits from employers, including health insurance, paid vacation and sick days, and retirement plans.

WORK ENVIRONMENT

Biomedical engineers who teach in a university will have much student contact in the classroom, the laboratory, and the office. They also will be expected to serve on relevant committees while continuing their teaching, research, and writing responsibilities. As competition for teaching positions increases, the requirement that professors publish papers will increase. Professors usually are responsible for obtaining government or private research grants to support their work.

Those who work in industry and government have much contact with other professionals, including chemists, medical scientists, and doctors. They often work as part of a team, testing and developing new products. All biomedical engineers who do lab work are in clean, well-lighted environments, using sophisticated equipment.

OUTLOOK

It is expected that there will be a greater need for skilled biomedical engineers in the future. Prospects look particularly good in the health care industry, which will continue to grow rapidly, primarily because people are living longer. The U.S. Department of Labor predicts employment for biomedical engineers to increase much faster than the average for all occupations through 2014. New jobs will become available in biomedical research in prosthetics, artificial internal organs, computer applications, and instrumentation and other medical systems. In addition, a demand will exist for professors to train the biomedical engineers needed to fill these positions.

FOR MORE INFORMATION

For more information on careers in biomedical engineering, contact
American Society for Engineering Education
1818 N Street, NW, Suite 600
Washington, DC 20036-2479
Tel: 202-331-3500
http://www.asee.org

For information on careers, student chapters, and to read the bro-chure, Planning a Career in Biomedical Engineering, *contact or visit the following Web site:*
Biomedical Engineering Society
8401 Corporate Drive, Suite 140
Landover, MD 20785-2224
Tel: 301-459-1999
Email: info@bmes.org
http://www.bmes.org

For information on high school programs that provide opportuni-ties to learn about engineering technology, contact JETS.
Junior Engineering Technical Society (JETS)
1420 King Street, Suite 405
Alexandria, VA 22314-2794
Tel: 703-548-5387
Email: info@jets.org
http://www.jets.org

For Canadian career information, contact
Canadian Medical and Biological Engineering Society
PO Box 51023
Orleans, ON K1E 3W4 Canada
Tel: 613-837-8649
Email: cmbes@magma.ca
http://www.cmbes.ca

Visit the following Web site for more information on educational programs, job listings, grants, and links to other biomedical engi-neering sites:
The Biomedical Engineering Network
http://www.bmenet.org

Chemical Engineers

OVERVIEW

Chemical engineers take chemistry out of the laboratory and into the real world. They are involved in evaluating methods and equipment for the mass production of chemicals and other materials requiring chemical processing. They also develop products from these materials, such as plastics, metals, gasoline, detergents, pharmaceuticals, and foodstuffs. They develop or improve safe, environmentally sound processes, determine the least costly production method, and formulate the material for easy use and safe, economic transportation. Approximately 31,000 chemical engineers work in the United States.

HISTORY

Chemical engineering, defined in its most general sense as applied chemistry, existed even in early civilizations. Ancient Greeks, for example, distilled alcoholic beverages, as did the Chinese, who by 800 B.C. had learned to distill alcohol from the fermentation of rice. Aristotle, a fourth-century B.C. Greek philosopher, wrote about a process for obtaining fresh water by evaporating and condensing water from the sea.

The foundations of modern chemical engineering were laid out during the Renaissance, when experimentation and the questioning of accepted scientific theories became widespread. This period saw the development of many new chemical processes, such as those for producing sulfuric acid (for fertilizers and textile treatment) and alkalies (for soap). The atomic theories of John Dalton and Amedeo

A chemical engineer (left) and agricultural engineer mill barley kernels into starch-enriched fractions for ethanol production and low-starch fractions for food and feed. *(Agricultural Research Service)*

Avogadro, developed in the 1800s, supplied the theoretical underpinning for modern chemistry and chemical engineering.

With the advent of large-scale manufacturing in the mid-19th century, modern chemical engineering began to take shape. Chemical manufacturers were soon required to seek out chemists familiar with manufacturing processes. These early chemical engineers were called chemical technicians or industrial chemists. The first course in chemical engineering was taught in 1888 at the Massachusetts Institute of Technology, and by 1900, "chemical engineer" had become a widely used job title.

Chemical engineers are employed in increasing numbers to design new and more efficient ways to produce chemicals and chemical by-products. In the United States, they have been especially important in the development of petroleum-based fuels for internal combustion engine-powered vehicles. Their achievements range from the large-scale production of plastics, antibiotics, and synthetic rubbers to the development of high-octane gasoline.

THE JOB

Chemical engineering is one of the four major engineering disciplines (the others are electrical, mechanical, and civil). Because chemical engineers are rigorously trained not only in chemistry but also in physics, mathematics, and other sciences such as biology or geology, they are among the most versatile of all engineers, with many specialties, and they are employed in many industries. Chemical industries, which transform raw materials into desired products, employ the largest number of chemical engineers.

There are many stages in the production of chemicals and related materials, and the following paragraphs describe specific jobs responsibilities by production stage for chemical engineers. At smaller companies, engineers may have a hand in all of these production phases, while job duties are more specialized in larger plants.

Research engineers work with chemists to develop new processes and products, or they may develop better methods to make existing products. Product ideas may originate with the company's marketing department; with a chemist, chemical engineer, or other specialist; or with a customer. The basic chemical process for the product is then developed in a laboratory, where various experiments are conducted to determine the process's viability. Some projects die here.

Others go on to be developed and refined at pilot plants, which are small-scale versions of commercial plants. Chemical engineers in these plants run tests on the processes and make any necessary modifications. They strive to improve the process, reduce safety hazards and waste, and cut production time and costs. Throughout the development stage, engineers keep detailed records of the proceedings, and they may abandon projects that aren't viable.

When a new process is judged to be viable, *process design engineers* determine how the product can most efficiently be produced on a large scale while still guaranteeing a consistently high-quality result. These engineers consider process requirements and cost, convenience and safety for the operators, waste minimization, legal regulations, and preservation of the environment. Besides working on the steps of the process, they also work on the design of the equipment to be used in the process. These chemical engineers are often assisted in plant and equipment design by mechanical, electrical, and civil engineers.

Project engineers oversee the construction of new plants and installation of new equipment. In construction, chemical engineers may work as *field engineers*, who are involved in the testing and initial operation of the equipment and assist in plant start-up and operator training. Once a process is fully implemented at a manufacturing plant, *production engineers* supervise the day-to-day operations. They are responsible for the rate of production, scheduling, worker safety, quality control, and other important operational concerns.

Chemical engineers working in environmental control are involved in waste management, recycling, and control of air and water pollution. They work with the engineers in research and development, process design, equipment and plant construction, and production to incorporate environmental protection measures into all stages of the chemical engineering process.

As *technical sales engineers,* chemical engineers may work with customers of manufactured products to determine what best fits their needs. They answer questions such as "Could our products be used more economically than those now in use? Why does this paint peel?" etc. Others work as managers, making policy and business decisions and overseeing the training of new personnel. The variety of job descriptions is almost limitless because of chemical engineers' versatility and adaptability.

REQUIREMENTS

High School

High school students interested in chemical engineering should take all the mathematics and science courses their schools offer. These should include algebra, geometry, calculus, trigonometry, chemistry, physics, and biology. Computer science courses are also highly recommended. In addition, students should take four years of English, and a foreign language is valuable. To enhance their desirability, students should participate in high school science and engineering clubs and other extracurricular activities.

Postsecondary Training

A bachelor's degree in chemical engineering is the minimum educational requirement for entering the field. For some positions, an M.S., an M.B.A., or a Ph.D. may be required. A Ph.D. may be essential for advancement in research, teaching, and administration.

For their college studies, students should attend a chemical engineering program approved by the Accreditation Board for Engineering and Technology and the American Institute of Chemical Engineers (AIChE). There are more than 150 accredited undergraduate programs in chemical engineering in the United States offering bachelor's degrees. Some engineering programs last five or six years; these often include work experience in industry.

As career plans develop, students should consult with advisors about special career paths in which they are interested. Those who want to teach or conduct research will need a graduate degree. There are approximately 140 accredited chemical engineering graduate programs in the United States. A master's degree generally takes two years of study beyond undergraduate school, while a Ph.D. program requires four to six years.

In graduate school, students specialize in one aspect of chemical engineering, such as chemical kinetics or biotechnology. Graduate education also helps to obtain promotions, and some companies offer tuition reimbursement to encourage employees to take graduate courses. For engineers who would like to become managers, a master's degree in business administration may be helpful. Chemical engineers must be prepared for a lifetime of education to keep up with the rapid advances in technology.

Certification or Licensing

Chemical engineers must be licensed as professional engineers if their work involves providing services directly to the public. All 50 states and the District of Columbia have specific licensing requirements, which include graduation from an accredited engineering school, passing a written exam, and having at least four years of engineering experience. About one-third of all chemical engineers are licensed; they are called registered engineers. For more information on licensing and examination requirements, visit http://www.ncees.org.

Other Requirements

Important personal qualities are honesty, accuracy, objectivity, and perseverance. In addition, chemical engineers must be inquisitive, open-minded, creative, and flexible. Problem-solving ability is essential. To remain competitive in the job market, they should display initiative and leadership skills, exhibit the ability to work well in teams and collaborate across disciplines, and be able to work with people of different linguistic and cultural backgrounds.

EXPLORING

High school students should join science clubs and take part in other extracurricular activities and join such organizations as the Junior Engineering Technical Society (JETS). JETS participants have opportunities to enter engineering design and problem-solving contests and to learn team development skills. Science contests are also a good way to apply principles learned in classes to a special project. Students can also subscribe to the American Chemical Society's *ChemMatters*, a quarterly magazine for high school chemistry students.

College students can join professional associations, such as the American Chemical Society (ACS), AIChE, and the Society of Manufacturing Engineers (composed of individual associations with specific fields of interest), as student affiliates. Membership benefits include subscription to magazines—some of them geared specifically toward students—that provide the latest industry information. College students can also contact ACS or AIChE local sections to arrange to talk with some chemical engineers about what they do. These associations can also help students find summer or co-op work experiences.

In addition, the Society of Women Engineers (SWE) has a mentor program in which high school and college women are matched with an SWE member in their area. This member is available to answer questions and provide a firsthand introduction to a career in engineering.

EMPLOYERS

There are approximately 31,000 chemical engineers working in the United States. While the many chemical engineers work in manufacturing industries, others are employed by federal and state governments, colleges and universities, and research and testing services. The list of individual employers, if cited, would take many pages. However, the following industry classifications indicate where most chemical engineers are employed: aerospace, fuels, electronics, food and consumer products, design and construction, materials, biotechnology, pharmaceuticals, environmental control, pulp and paper, public utilities, and consultation firms. Because of the nature of their training and background, chemical engineers can easily obtain employment with another company in a completely different field if necessary or desired.

STARTING OUT

Most chemical engineers obtain their first position through company recruiters sent to college campuses. Others may find employment with companies with whom they have had summer or work-study arrangements. Many respond to advertisements in professional journals or newspapers. The Internet now offers multiple opportunities to job seekers, and many libraries have programs that offer assistance in making use of the available job listings. Chemical engineers may also contact colleges and universities regarding positions as part-time teaching or laboratory assistants if they wish to continue study for a graduate degree. Student members of professional societies often use the employment services of these organizations, including resume data banks, online job listings, national employment clearinghouses, and employers' mailing lists.

Typically, new recruits begin as trainees or process engineers. They often begin work under the supervision of seasoned engineers. Many participate in special training programs designed to orient them to company processes, procedures, policies, and products. This allows the company to determine where the new personnel may best fulfill their needs. After this training period, new employees often rotate positions to get an all-around experience in working for the company.

ADVANCEMENT

Entry-level personnel usually advance to project or production engineers after learning the ropes in product manufacturing. They may then be assigned to sales and marketing. A large percentage of engineers no longer do engineering work by the 10th year of their employment. At that point, they often advance to supervisory or management positions. An M.B.A. enhances their opportunities for promotion. A doctoral degree is essential for university teaching or supervisory research positions. Some engineers may decide at this point that they prefer to start their own consulting firms. Continued advancement, raises, and increased responsibility are not automatic but depend on sustained demonstration of leadership skills.

EARNINGS

Though starting salaries have dipped somewhat in recent years, chemical engineering is still one of the highest paid scientific professions. Salaries vary with education, experience, industry, and employer. The U.S. Department of Labor reports that the median annual salary for chemical engineers was $77,140 in 2005. The lowest paid 10 percent earned less than $49,350; the highest paid 10 percent earned more than $113,950 annually. According to a 2005 salary survey by the National Association of Colleges and Employers, starting annual salaries for those with bachelor's degrees in chemical engineering averaged $53,813; with master's degrees, $57,260; and Ph.D's, $79,591. Chemical engineers with doctoral degrees and many years of experience in supervisory and management positions may have salaries exceeding $100,000 annually.

Benefits offered depend on the employer; however, chemical engineers typically receive such things as paid vacation and sick days, health insurance, and retirement plans.

WORK ENVIRONMENT

Because the industries in which chemical engineers work are so varied—from academia to waste treatment and disposal—the working conditions also vary. Most chemical engineers work in clean, well-maintained offices, laboratories, or plants, although some occasionally work outdoors, particularly construction engineers. Travel to new or existing plants may be required. Some chemical engineers work with dangerous chemicals, but the adoption of safe working practices has greatly reduced potential health hazards. Chemical engineers at institutions of higher learning spend their time in classrooms or research laboratories.

The workweek for a chemical engineer in manufacturing is usually 40 hours, although many work longer hours. Because plants often operate around the clock, they may work different shifts or have irregular hours.

OUTLOOK

The U.S. Department of Labor projects that employment for chemical engineers will grow about as fast as the average for all occupations through 2014. Certain areas of the field will offer more job opportunities than others. Chemical and pharmaceutical companies, for example, will need engineers in research and development to work on new chemicals and more efficient processes. Additionally, growth will come in service industries, such as companies providing research and testing services. Job opportunities will be best in the energy, biotechnology, and nanotechnology segments of this industry sector.

FOR MORE INFORMATION

For information on undergraduate internships, summer jobs, and co-op programs, contact
American Chemical Society
1155 16th Street, NW
Washington, DC 20036-4801
Tel: 800-227-5558
Email: help@acs.org
http://www.chemistry.org

For information on awards, accredited programs, internships, student chapters, and career opportunities, contact
American Institute of Chemical Engineers
Three Park Avenue
New York, NY 10016-5991
Tel: 800-242-4363
http://www.aiche.org

For information about programs, products, and a chemical engineering career brochure, contact
Junior Engineering Technical Society
1420 King Street, Suite 405
Alexandria, VA 22314-2794
Tel: 703-548-5387
Email: info@jets.org
http://www.jets.org

For information on National Engineers Week Programs held in many U.S. locations, contact
National Engineers Week Headquarters
1420 King Street
Alexandria, VA 22314-2794
Tel: 703-684-2852
Email: eweek@nspe.org
http://www.eweek.org

For information on training programs, seminars, and how to become a student member, contact
Society of Manufacturing Engineers
One SME Drive
Dearborn, MI 48121-2408
Tel: 800-733-4763
Email: service@sme.org
http://www.sme.org

For information on career guidance literature, scholarships, and mentor programs, contact
Society of Women Engineers
230 East Ohio Street, Suite 400
Chicago, IL 60611-3265
Tel: 312-596-5223
Email: hq@swe.org
http://www.swe.org

─── INTERVIEW ───

Dr. Jennifer Wilcox is a chemical engineer and an assistant professor of chemical engineering at Worcester Polytechnic Institute in Worcester, Massachusetts. She discussed her career with the editors of Careers in Focus: Engineering.

Q. Why did you decide to become a chemical engineer?

A. Chemical engineering is a field that crosses many disciplines, requiring a solid foundation in mathematics and chemistry to develop new ideas and novel solutions to applications within fields such as environmental chemistry, materials science, and nanotechnology. As an undergraduate at Wellesley College I majored in mathematics, but obtained a strong background in chemistry from completing the premed sequence. With a personal interest in pursuing a career that involves projects with environmental applications, it seemed logical to use these fundamental strengths to explore a career in chemical engineering.

Q. Tell us about your research and career interests.

A. My research team has ongoing investigations in several areas ranging from applications in combustion reaction engineering to membrane design for hydrogen storage and separation. Within combustion reaction engineering, our team is simulating combustion flue gases through both experiments and computational modeling to determine the speciation of trace elements of mercury, arsenic, and selenium. Efforts are also focused on using computational chemistry to model and design novel sorbents for trace element capture. Further, our team is using computational chemistry and modeling to determine properties of palladium-based membranes for the separation of hydrogen for the use in fuel cells.

In addition to graduate students, there are several undergraduates who work in the lab each year. In fact, through collaborations with universities abroad in locations such as Bangkok, Thailand, our undergraduate students have the opportunity to carry out research in a completely unique environment. Additionally, our research team is involved with high school outreach activities through incorporating computational chemistry and molecular modeling into the development of new software designed to assist high school science teachers in reaching a broader range of students in the classroom.

Q. **What advice would you give to high school students who are interested in this career?**

A. If a high school student has an interest in chemical engineering, I would urge the student to continue studying fundamental concepts in chemistry and physics with mathematics as a guide and to pursue fundamental texts such as *Six Easy Pieces: Essentials of Physics Explained by Its Most Brilliant Teacher,* written by Richard Feynman. To develop unique and novel ideas and to invent through engineering, the scholar needs to understand concepts from a fundamental level; this understanding and learning should ideally take place during junior high or high school. Do not limit yourself to a text which includes a single author, but rather seek out the original scientists of a theory or narrow field that interests you and read their original writings. Oftentimes Nobel laureate lectures from the early 1900s are a good start. Recent authors tend to teach topics in a condensed format, leaving out the details that are required for a true and subsequent pure understanding of a given topic.

It is a common misconception that writing and critical thinking are not necessary skills to ensure a successful career in engineering. However, having strengths in these areas provides the engineer with the ability to communicate their ideas in an

effective and efficient manner, which aids in promoting a fundamental understanding and knowledge base of a given topic.

**Q. What are the most important personal qualities for
chemical engineering majors?**

A. Chemical engineering is a field that spans multiple disciplines,
and students beginning their studies within this field should gain
comfort in reading material within physical, chemical, biological, materials science, and environmental applications. When
chemical engineering majors are beginning their introductory
coursework they should be aware that the tools being learned
can be applied to multiple problems, each with a unique history and context to one another. This interdisciplinary nature
of chemical engineering requires the scientist to be an effective
communicator and teacher, constantly reaching out to a broad
and, hence, diverse population. Therefore, the best qualities
for an engineer would be for them to have an open mind, try
to make connections to applications, and to be well rounded
for gaining knowledge in various areas within the field.

**Q. How will the field of chemical engineering change in the
future?**

A. Currently chemical engineering is moving away from the traditional image involving careers in petroleum refining and is
moving toward applications involving biotechnology, materials
science, environmental chemistry, etc. The field is changing
in that it will continue to be a discipline that involves many
choices for those wishing to pursue a career in this multidisci-
plinary field.

Civil Engineers

OVERVIEW

Civil engineers are involved in the design and construction of the physical structures that make up our surroundings, such as roads, bridges, buildings, and harbors. Civil engineering involves theoretical knowledge applied to the practical planning of the layout of our cities, towns, and other communities. It is concerned with modifying the natural environment and building new environments to better the lifestyles of the general public. Civil engineers are also known as *structural engineers*. There are approximately 237,000 civil engineers in the United States.

HISTORY

One might trace the evolution of civil engineering methods by considering the building and many reconstructions of England's London Bridge. In Roman and medieval times, several bridges made of timber were built over the Thames River. Around the end of the 12th century, these were rebuilt into 19 narrow arches mounted on piers. A chapel was built on one of the piers, and two towers were built for defense. A fire damaged the bridge around 1212, yet the surrounding area was considered a preferred place to live and work, largely because it was the only bridge over which one could cross the river. The structure was rebuilt many times during later centuries using different materials and designs. By 1830, it had only five arches. More than a century later, the center span of the bridge was remodeled, and part of it was actually transported to the United States to be set up as a tourist attraction.

Working materials for civil engineers have changed during many centuries. For instance, bridges, once made of timber, then of iron

QUICK FACTS

School Subjects
Mathematics
Physics

Personal Skills
Leadership/management
Technical/scientific

Work Environment
Indoors and outdoors
Primarily multiple locations

Minimum Education Level
Bachelor's degree

Salary Range
$43,679 to $66,190 to
$100,040+

Certification or Licensing
Recommended

Outlook
About as fast as the average

DOT
055

GOE
05.01.07

NOC
2131

O*NET-SOC
17-2051.00

A civil engineer and contractor discuss design changes at a construction site. *(Index Stock Imagery)*

and steel, are today made mainly with concrete that is reinforced with steel. The high strength of the material is necessary because of the abundance of cars and other heavy vehicles that travel over the bridges.

As the population continues to grow and communities become more complex, structures that civil engineers must pay attention to have to be remodeled and repaired. New highways, buildings, airstrips, and so forth must be designed to accommodate public needs. Today, more and more civil engineers are involved with water treatment plants, water purification plants, and toxic waste sites. Increasing concern about the natural environment is also evident in the growing number of engineers working on such projects as preservation of wetlands, maintenance of national forests, and restoration of sites around land mines, oil wells, and industrial factories.

THE JOB

Civil engineers use their knowledge of materials science, engineering theory, economics, and demographics to devise, construct, and maintain our physical surroundings. They apply their understanding of other branches of science—such as hydraulics, geology, and physics—to design the optimal blueprint for the project.

Feasibility studies are conducted by *surveying and mapping engineers* to determine the best sites and approaches for construction. They extensively investigate the chosen sites to verify that the ground and other surroundings are amenable to the proposed project. These engineers use sophisticated equipment, such as satellites and other electronic instruments, to measure the area and conduct underground probes for bedrock and groundwater. They determine the optimal places where explosives should be blasted in order to cut through rock.

Many civil engineers work strictly as consultants on projects, advising their clients. These consultants usually specialize in one area of the industry, such as water systems, transportation systems, or housing structures. Clients include individuals, corporations, and the government. Consultants will devise an overall design for the proposed project, perhaps a nuclear power plant commissioned by an electric company. They will estimate the cost of constructing the plant, supervise the feasibility studies and site investigations, and advise the client on whom to hire for the actual labor involved. Consultants are also responsible for such details as accuracy of drawings and quantities of materials to order.

Other civil engineers work mainly as contractors and are responsible for the actual building of the structure; they are known as *construction engineers*. They interpret the consultants' designs and follow through with the best methods for getting the work done, usually working directly at the construction site. Contractors are responsible for scheduling the work, buying the materials, maintaining surveys of the progress of the work, and choosing the machines and other equipment used for construction. During construction, these civil engineers must supervise the labor and make sure the work is completed correctly and efficiently. After the project is finished, they must set up a maintenance schedule and periodically check the structure for a certain length of time. Later, the task of ongoing maintenance and repair is often transferred to local engineers.

Civil engineers may be known by their area of specialization. *Transportation engineers*, for example, are concerned mainly with the construction of highways and mass transit systems, such as subways and commuter rail lines. When devising plans for subways, engineers are responsible for considering the tunneling that is involved. *Pipeline engineers* are specialized civil engineers who are involved with the movement of water, oil, and gas through miles of pipeline.

REQUIREMENTS

High School

Because a bachelor's degree is considered essential in the field, high school students interested in civil engineering must follow a college prep curriculum. Students should focus on mathematics (algebra, trigonometry, geometry, and calculus), the sciences (physics and chemistry), computer science, and English and the humanities (history, economics, and sociology). Students should also aim for honors-level courses.

Postsecondary Training

In addition to completing the core engineering curriculum (including mathematics, science, drafting, and computer applications), students can choose their specialty from the following types of courses: structural analysis; materials design and specification; geology; hydraulics; surveying and design graphics; soil mechanics; and oceanography. Bachelor's degrees can be achieved through a number of programs: a four- or five-year accredited college or university; two years in a community college engineering program plus two or three years in a college or university; or five or six years in a co-op program (attending classes for part of the year and working in an engineering-related job for the rest of the year). About 30 percent of civil engineering students go on to receive a master's degree.

Certification or Licensing

Most civil engineers go on to study and qualify for a professional engineer (PE) license. It is required before one can work on projects affecting property, health, or life. Because many engineering jobs are found in government specialties, most engineers take the necessary steps to obtain the license. Requirements are different for each state—they involve educational, practical, and teaching experience. Applicants must take an examination on a specified date. For more information on licensing and examination requirements, visit http://www.ncees.org.

Other Requirements

Basic personal characteristics often found in civil engineers are an avid curiosity; a passion for mathematics and science; an aptitude for problem solving, both alone and with a team; and an ability to visualize multidimensional, spatial relationships.

EXPLORING

High school students can become involved in civil engineering by attending a summer camp or study program in the field. For example, the Worcester Polytechnic Institute in Massachusetts has a summer program for high school students who have completed their junior year and will be entering their senior year in the fall. Studies and events focus on science and math and include specialties for those interested in civil engineering.

After high school, another way to learn about civil engineering duties is to work on a construction crew that is involved in the actual building of a project designed and supervised by engineers. Such hands-on experience would provide an opportunity to work near many types of civil workers. Try to work on highway crews or even in housing construction.

EMPLOYERS

Nearly half of all civil engineers work for companies involved in architectural and engineering consulting services. Others work for government agencies at the local, state, or federal level. A small percentage are self-employed, running their own consulting businesses. Approximately 237,000 civil engineers work in the United States.

STARTING OUT

To establish a career as a civil engineer, one must first receive a bachelor's degree in engineering or another appropriate scientific field. College career services offices are often the best sources of employment for beginning engineers. Entry-level jobs usually involve routine work, often as a member of a supervised team. After a year or more (depending on job performance and qualifications), one becomes a junior engineer, then an assistant to perhaps one or more supervising engineers. Establishment as a professional engineer comes after passing the PE exam.

ADVANCEMENT

Professional engineers with many years' experience often join with partners to establish their own firms in design, consulting, or contracting. Some leave long-held positions to be assigned as top executives in industries such as manufacturing and business consulting. Also, there are those who return to academia to teach high school or college students. For all of these potential opportunities, it is necessary to keep abreast of engineering advancements and trends by reading industry journals and taking courses.

EARNINGS

Civil engineers are among the lowest paid in the engineering field; however, their salaries are high when compared to those of many other occupations. The median annual earnings for civil engineers were $66,190 in 2005, according to the U.S. Department of Labor. The lowest paid 10 percent made less than $44,410 per year, and, at the other end of the pay scale, 10 percent earned more than $100,040 annually. Civil engineers working for the federal government had a mean salary of $77,230 in 2005. According to a 2005 survey by the National Association of Colleges and Employers, starting salaries by degree level averaged as follows: bachelor's, $43,679; master's, $48,050; and doctorate, $59,625. As with all occupations, salaries are higher for those with more experience.

Benefits typically include such extras as health insurance, retirement plans, and paid vacation days.

WORK ENVIRONMENT

Many civil engineers work regular 40-hour weeks, often in or near major industrial and commercial areas. Sometimes they are assigned to work in remote areas and foreign countries. Because of the diversity of civil engineering positions, working conditions vary widely. Offices, labs, factories, and actual sites are typical environments for engineers. About one-third of all civil engineers can be found working for various levels of government, usually involving large public-works projects, such as highways and bridges.

A typical work cycle involving various types of civil engineers involves three stages: planning, constructing, and maintaining. Those involved with development of a campus compound, for example, would first need to work in their offices developing plans for a survey. Surveying and mapping engineers would have to visit the proposed site to take measurements and perhaps shoot aerial photographs. The measurements and photos would have to be converted into drawings and blueprints. Geotechnical engineers would dig wells at the site and take core samples from the ground. If toxic waste or unexpected water is found at the site, the contractor determines what should be done.

Actual construction then begins. Very often, a field trailer on the site becomes the engineers' makeshift offices. The campus might take several years to build—it is not uncommon for engineers to be involved in long-term projects. If contractors anticipate that deadlines will not be met, they often put in weeks of 10- to 15-hour days on the job.

After construction is complete, engineers spend less and less time at the site. Some may be assigned to stay on-site to keep daily surveys of how the structure is holding up and to solve problems when they arise. Eventually, the project engineers finish the job and move on to another long-term assignment.

OUTLOOK

Employment for civil engineers is expected to grow about as fast as the average for all occupations through 2014, according to the U.S. Department of Labor. Employment will come from the need to maintain and repair public works, such as highways, bridges, and water systems, as well as improve infrastructure security. In addition, as the population grows, so does the need for more transportation and pollution control systems, which creates jobs for those who construct these systems. Firms providing management consulting and computer services may also be sources of jobs for civil engineers. However, employment is affected by several factors, including decisions made by the government to spend further on renewing and adding to the country's basic infrastructure and the health of the economy in general.

FOR MORE INFORMATION

For information on careers and scholarships, contact
American Society of Civil Engineers
1801 Alexander Bell Drive
Reston, VA 20191-4400
Tel: 800-548-2723
http://www.asce.org

Frontiers is a program for high school seniors that covers science material not traditionally offered in high school. For information, contact
Frontiers - Worcester Polytechnic Institute
100 Institute Road
Worcester, MA 01609-2280
Tel: 508-831-5286
Email: frontiers@wpi.edu
http://www.wpi.edu/Admin/AO/Frontiers

For information on careers and colleges and universities with ITE student chapters, contact
Institute of Transportation Engineers (ITE)
1099 14th Street, NW, Suite 300 West
Washington, DC 20005-3438

Tel: 202-289-0222
Email: ite_staff@ite.org
http://www.ite.org

The JETS offers high school students the opportunity to try engineering through a number of programs and competitions. To find out more about these opportunities or for general career information, contact

Junior Engineering Technical Society
1420 King Street, Suite 405
Alexandria, VA 22314-2794
Tel: 703-548-5387
Email: info@jets.org
http://www.jets.org

Electrical and Electronics Engineers

OVERVIEW

Electrical engineers apply their knowledge of the sciences to working with equipment that produces and distributes electricity, such as generators, transmission lines, and transformers. They also design, develop, and manufacture electric motors, electrical machinery, and ignition systems for automobiles, aircraft, and other engines. *Electronics engineers* are more concerned with devices made up of electronic components such as integrated circuits and microprocessors. They design, develop, and manufacture products such as computers, telephones, and radios. Electronics engineering is a subfield of electrical engineering, and both types of engineers are often referred to as electrical engineers. There are approximately 299,000 electrical and electronics engineers employed in the United States.

HISTORY

Electrical and electronics engineering had their true beginnings in the 19th century. In 1800, Alexander Volta made a discovery that opened a door to the science of electricity—he found that electric current could be harnessed and made to flow. By the mid-1800s the basic rules of electricity were established, and the first practical applications appeared. At that time, Michael Faraday discovered the phenomenon of electromagnetic induction. Further discoveries followed. In 1837 Samuel Morse invented the telegraph; in 1876 Alexander Graham Bell invented the telephone; the incandescent lamp (the light bulb) was invented by Thomas Edison in 1878; and the first electric motor was invented by Nicholas Tesla in 1888 (Faraday had built a primitive model of one in 1821). These inventions required the further generation and harnessing of electricity, so efforts were concentrated on developing ways to produce more and more power and to create better equipment, such as motors and transformers.

Edison's invention led to a dependence on electricity for lighting our homes, work areas, and streets. He later created the phonograph and other electrical instruments, leading to the establishment of his General Electric Company. One of today's major telephone companies also had its beginnings during this time. Alexander Bell's invention led to the establishment of the Bell Telephone Company, which eventually became American Telephone and Telegraph (AT&T).

The roots of electronics, which is distinguished from the science of electricity by its focus on lower power generation, can also be found in the 19th century. In the late 1800s, current moving through space was observed for the first time; this was called the "Edison effect." In the early 20th century, devices (such as vacuum tubes, which are pieces of metal inside a glass bulb) were invented that could transmit weak electrical signals, leading to the potential transmission of electromagnetic waves for communication, or radio broadcast. The unreliability of vacuum tubes led to the invention of equipment that could pass electricity through solid materials; hence transistors came to be known as solid-state devices.

In the 1960s, transistors were being built on tiny bits of silicon, creating the microchip. The computer industry is a major beneficiary of the creation of these circuits, because vast amounts of information can be stored on just one tiny chip smaller than a dime.

The invention of microchips led to the development of microprocessors. Microprocessors are silicon chips on which the logic and arithmetic functions of a computer are placed. Microprocessors serve as miniature computers and are used in many types of products. The miniaturization of electronic components allowed scientists and engineers to make smaller, lighter computers that could perform the same, or additional, functions of larger computers. They also allowed for the development of many new products. At first they were used primarily in desktop calculators, video games, digital watches, telephones, and microwave ovens. Today, microprocessors are used in electronic controls of automobiles, personal computers, telecommunications systems, and many other products. As a leader in advanced technology, the electronics industry is one of the most important industries today.

THE JOB

Because electrical and electronics engineering is such a diverse field, there are numerous divisions within which engineers work. In fact, the discipline reaches nearly every other field of applied science and technology. In general, electrical and electronics engineers use their knowledge of the sciences in the practical applications of electrical energy. They concern themselves with things as large as atom smashers and as small as microchips. They are involved in the invention, design, construction, and operation of electrical and electronic systems and devices of all kinds.

The work of electrical and electronics engineers touches almost every niche of our lives. Think of the things around you that have been designed, manufactured, maintained, or in any other way affected by electrical energy: the lights in a room, cars on the road, televisions, stereo systems, telephones, your doctor's blood-pressure reader, computers. When you start to think in these terms, you will discover that the electrical engineer has in some way had a hand in science, industry, commerce, entertainment, and even art.

The list of specialties that engineers are associated with reads like an alphabet of scientific titles—from acoustics, speech, and signal processing; to electromagnetic compatibility; geoscience and remote sensing; lasers and electro-optics; robotics; ultrasonics, ferroelectrics, and frequency control; to vehicular technology. As evident in this selected list, engineers are apt to specialize in what interests them, such as communications, robotics, or automobiles.

As mentioned earlier, electrical engineers focus on high-power generation of electricity and how it is transmitted for use in lighting homes and powering factories. They are also concerned with how equipment is designed and maintained and how communications are transmitted via wire and airwaves. Some are involved in the design and construction of power plants and the manufacture and maintenance of industrial machinery.

Electronics engineers work with smaller-scale applications, such as how computers are wired, how appliances work, or how electrical circuits are used in an endless number of applications. They may specialize in computers, industrial equipment and controls, aerospace equipment, or biomedical equipment.

Tom Busch is an electrical engineer for the U.S. government. He works at the Naval Surface Warfare Center, Crane Division, and much of his work involves testing equipment that will be used on the navy's ships. "We get equipment that government contractors have put together and test it to make sure it is functioning correctly before it goes out to the fleet," he says. "The type of equipment we test might be anything from navigation to propulsion to communications equipment." Although much of his work currently focuses on testing, Busch also does design work. "We do some software design and also design circuits that go in weapons systems," he says.

Design and testing are only two of several categories in which electrical and electronics engineers may find their niche. Others include research and development, production, field service, sales and marketing, and teaching. In addition, even within each category there are divisions of labor.

Researchers concern themselves mainly with issues that pertain to potential applications. They conduct tests and perform studies to evaluate fundamental problems involving such things as new materials and chemical interactions. Those who work in design and development adapt the researchers' findings to actual practical applications. They devise functioning devices and draw up plans for their efficient production, using computer-aided design and engineering (CAD/CAE) tools. For a typical product such as a television, this phase usually takes up to 18 months to accomplish. For other products, particularly those that utilize developing technology, this phase can take as long as 10 years or more.

Production engineers have perhaps the most hands-on tasks in the field. They are responsible for the organization of the actual manufacture of whatever electric product is being made. They take care of materials and machinery, schedule technicians and assembly workers, and make sure that standards are met and products are quality controlled. These engineers must have access to the best tools for measurement, materials handling, and processing.

After electrical systems are put in place, *field service engineers* must act as the liaison between the manufacturer or distributor and the client. They ensure the correct installation, operation, and maintenance of systems and products for both industry and individuals. In the sales and marketing divisions, engineers stay abreast of customer needs in order to evaluate potential applications, and they advise their companies of orders and effective marketing. A *sales engineer* would contact a client interested in, say, a certain type of microchip for its automobile electrical system controls. He or she would learn about the client's needs and report back to the various engineering teams at his or her company. During the manufacture and distribution of the product, the sales engineer would continue to communicate information between company and client until all objectives were met.

All engineers must be taught their skills, and so it is important that some remain involved in academia. *Professors* usually teach a portion of the basic engineering courses as well as classes in the subjects that they specialize in. Conducting personal research is generally an ongoing task for professors in addition to the supervision of student work and student research. A part of the teacher's time is also devoted to providing career and academic guidance to students.

Whatever type of project an engineer works on, he or she is likely to have a certain amount of desk work. Writing status reports and communicating with clients and others who are working on the same project are examples of the paperwork that most engineers are responsible for. Busch says that the amount of time he spends doing desk work varies from project to project. "Right now, I probably spend about half of my time in the lab and half at my desk," he says. "But it varies, really. Sometimes, I'm hardly in the lab at all; other times, I'm hardly at my desk."

REQUIREMENTS

High School

Electrical and electronics engineers must have a solid educational background, and the discipline requires a clear understanding of practical applications. To prepare for college, high school students should take classes in algebra, trigonometry, calculus, biology, physics, chemistry, computer science, word processing, English, and social studies. According to Tom Busch, business classes are also a good idea. "It wouldn't hurt to get some business understanding—and computer skills are tremendously important for engineers, as well," he says. Students who are planning to pursue studies beyond a bachelor of science degree will also need to take a foreign language. It is recommended that students aim for honors-level courses.

Postsecondary Training

Busch's educational background includes a bachelor of science degree in electrical engineering. Other engineers might receive similar degrees in electronics, computer engineering, or another related science. Numerous colleges and universities offer electrical, electronics, and computer engineering programs. Because the programs vary from one school to another, you should explore as many schools as possible to determine which program is most suited to your academic and personal interests and needs. Most engineering programs have strict admission requirements and require students to have excellent academic records and top scores on national college-entrance examinations. Competition can be fierce for some programs, and high school students are encouraged to apply early.

Many students go on to receive a master of science degree in a specialization of their choice. This usually takes an additional two years of study beyond a bachelor's program. Some students pursue a master's degree immediately upon completion of a bachelor's degree. Other students, however, gain work experience first and then take graduate-level courses on a part-time basis while they are employed. A Ph.D., is also available. It generally requires four years of study and research beyond the bachelor's degree and is usually completed by people interested in research or teaching.

By the time you reach college, it is wise to be considering which type of engineering specialty you might be interested in. In addition to the core engineering curriculum (advanced mathematics, physical science, engineering science, mechanical drawing, computer applications), students will begin to choose from the following types of courses: circuits and electronics, signals and systems, digital electronics and computer architecture, electromagnetic waves, systems, and machinery, communications, and statistical mechanics.

Certification or Licensing

Electrical and electronics engineers who work on projects that affect the property, health, or life of the public typically pursue licensure. There are two levels of licensing for engineers. Professional Engineers (PEs) have graduated from an accredited engineering curriculum, have four years of engineering experience, and have passed a written exam. Engineering graduates need not wait until they have four years experience, however, to start the licensure process. Those who pass the Fundamentals of Engineering examination after graduating are called Engineers-in-Training (EITs) or Engineer Interns (EIs). The EIT certification usually is valid for 10 years. After acquiring suitable work experience, EITs can take the second examination, the Principles and Practice of Engineering exam, to gain full PE licensure. For more information on licensing and examination requirements, visit http://www.ncees.org.

Other Requirements

To be a good electrical or electronics engineer, you should have strong problem-solving abilities, mathematical and scientific aptitudes, and the willingness to learn throughout one's career. According to Busch, a curiosity for how things work is also important. "I think you have to like to learn about things," he says. "I also think it helps to be kind of creative, to like to make things."

Most engineers work on teams with other professionals, and the ability to get along with others is essential. In addition, strong communications skills are needed. Engineers need to be able to write reports and give oral presentations.

EXPLORING

People who are interested in the excitement of electricity can tackle experiments such as building a radio or central processing unit of a computer. Special assignments can also be researched and supervised by teachers. Joining a science club, such as the Junior Engineering Technical Society (JETS), can provide hands-on activities and opportunities to explore scientific topics in depth. Student members can join competitions and design structures that exhibit scientific know-how. Reading trade publications, such as the *Pre-Engineering Times*, are other ways to learn about the engineering field. This magazine includes articles on engineering-related careers and club activities.

Students can also learn more about electrical and electronics engineering by attending a summer camp or academic program that focuses on scientific projects as well as recreational activities. For example, the Delphian School in Oregon holds summer sessions for high school students. Students are involved in leadership activities and special interests such as computers. Sports and wilderness activities are also offered. Summer programs such as the one offered by the Michigan Technological University focus on career exploration in computers, electronics, and robotics. This academic program for high school students also offers arts guidance, wilderness events, and other recreational activities. (For further information on clubs and programs, contact the sources listed at the end of this article.)

EMPLOYERS

Approximately 299,000 electrical and electronics engineers are employed in the United States. More engineers work in the electrical and electronics field than in any other division of engineering. Most work in engineering and business consulting firms, manufacturing companies that produce electrical and electronic equipment, business machines, computers and data processing companies, and telecommunications parts. Others work for companies that make automotive electronics, scientific equipment, and aircraft parts; consulting firms; public utilities; and government agencies. Some work as private consultants.

STARTING OUT

Many students begin to research companies that they are interested in working for during their last year of college or even before. It is possible to research companies using many resources, such as company directories and annual reports, available at public libraries. For example, *The Career Guide, Dun's Employment Opportunity Directory* lists companies that employ people in electrical/electronics engineering positions, as well as other careers. It gives brief company profiles, describes employment opportunities within the company, and provides addresses to which applicants can write.

Employment opportunities can be found through a variety of sources. Many engineers are recruited by companies while they are still in college. This is what happened to Tom Busch. "I was interviewed while I was still on campus, and I was hired for the job before I graduated," he says. Other companies have internship, work-study, or cooperative education programs from which they hire students who are still in college. Students who have participated in these programs often receive permanent job offers through these companies, or they may obtain useful contacts that can lead to a job interview or offer. Some companies use employment agencies and state employment offices. Companies may also advertise positions through advertisements in newspapers and trade publications. In addition, many newsletters and associations post job listings on the Internet.

Interested applicants can also apply directly to a company for which they are interested in working. A letter of interest and resume can be sent to the director of engineering or the head of a specific department. One may also apply to the personnel or human resources departments.

ADVANCEMENT

Engineering careers usually offer many avenues for advancement. An engineer straight out of college will usually take a job as an entry-level engineer and advance to higher positions after acquiring some job experience and technical skills. Engineers with strong technical skills who show leadership ability and good communications skills may move into positions that involve supervising teams of engineers and making sure they are working efficiently. Engineers can advance from these positions to that of a *chief engineer*. The chief engineer usually oversees all projects and has authority over project managers and managing engineers.

Many companies provide structured programs to train new employees and prepare them for advancement. These programs usually rely heavily on formal training opportunities such as in-house development programs and seminars. Some companies also provide special programs through colleges, universities, and outside agencies. Engineers usually advance from junior-level engineering positions to more senior-level positions through a series of positions. Engineers may also specialize in a specific area once they have acquired the necessary experience and skills.

Some engineers move into sales and managerial positions, with some engineers leaving the electronics industry to seek top-level management positions with other types of firms. Other engineers set up their own firms in design or consulting. Engineers can also move into the academic field and become teachers at high schools or universities.

The key to advancing in the electronics field is keeping pace with technological changes, which occur rapidly in this field. Electrical and electronics engineers will need to pursue additional training throughout their careers in order to stay up-to-date on new technologies and techniques.

EARNINGS

Starting salaries for all engineers are generally much higher than for workers in any other field. Entry-level electrical and electronics engineers with a bachelor's degree earned an average of $51,888, according to a 2005 salary survey by the National Association of Colleges and Employers. Electrical and electronics engineers with a master's degree averaged around $64,416 in their first jobs after graduation, and with a Ph.D. received average starting offers of $80,206. The U.S. Department of Labor reports that the median annual salary for electrical engineers was $73,510 in 2005. The lowest paid 10 percent of electrical engineers earned less than $47,750 and those in the top 10 percent of their fields earned more than $110,570 annually. Electronics engineers had median annual earnings of $78,030 in 2005. Salaries ranged from less than $50,090 to $114,630 or more annually.

Most companies offer attractive benefits packages, although the actual benefits vary from company to company. Benefits can include any of the following: paid holidays, paid vacations, personal days, sick leave; medical, health, life insurance; short- and long-term disability insurance; profit sharing; 401(k) plans; retirement and pension plans; educational assistance; leave time for educational purposes;

and credit unions. Some companies also offer computer purchase assistance plans and discounts on company products.

WORK ENVIRONMENT

Tom Busch's work hours are typically regular—9:00 to 5:00, Monday through Friday—although there is occasional overtime. In many parts of the country, this five-day, 40-hour workweek is still the norm, but it is becoming much less common. Many engineers regularly work 10 or 20 hours of overtime a week. Engineers in research and development, or those conducting experiments, often need to work at night or on weekends. Workers who supervise production activities may need to come in during the evenings or on weekends to handle special production requirements. In addition to the time spent on the job, many engineers also participate in professional associations and pursue additional training during their free time. Many high-tech companies allow flex-time, which means that workers can arrange their own schedules within certain time frames.

Most electrical and electronics engineers work in fairly comfortable environments. Engineers involved in research and design may, like Busch, work in specially equipped laboratories. Engineers involved in development and manufacturing work in offices and may spend part of their time in production facilities. Depending on the type of work one does, there may be extensive travel. Engineers involved in field service and sales spend a significant time traveling to see clients. Engineers working for large corporations may travel to other plants and manufacturing companies, both around the country and at foreign locations.

Engineering professors spend part of their time teaching in classrooms, part of it doing research either in labs or libraries, and some of the time still connected with industry.

OUTLOOK

The demand for electrical and electronics engineers fluctuates with changes in the economy. In the early 1990s, many companies that produced defense products suffered from cutbacks in defense orders and, as a result, made reductions in their engineering staffs. However, opportunities in defense-related fields have improved, as there is a growing trend toward upgrading existing aircraft and weapons systems. In addition, the increased use of electronic components in automobiles and medical electronics and increases in computer and telecommunications production require a high number of skilled engineers. Opportunities for electrical and electronics engineers are expected to increase about as fast as the average for all occupations through 2014, according to the *Occupational Outlook Handbook*. Although demand for electronics should increase, competition from foreign countries will tend to limit job growth for electrical and electronics engineers in the United States. The growing consumer, business, and government demand for improved computers and communications equipment is expected to propel much of this expected growth. Another area of high demand is projected to be the development of electrical and electronic goods for the consumer market. The strongest job growth, however, is likely to be in nonmanufacturing industries. This is because more and more firms are contracting for electronic engineering services from consulting and service firms.

Engineers will need to stay on top of changes within the electronics industry and will need additional training throughout their careers to learn new technologies. Economic trends and conditions within the global marketplace have become increasingly more important. In the past, most electronics production was done in the United States or by American-owned companies. During the 1990s, this changed, and the electronics industry entered an era of global production. Worldwide economies and production trends will have a larger impact on U.S. production, and companies that cannot compete technologically may not succeed. Job security is no longer a sure thing, and many engineers can expect to make significant changes in their careers at least once. Engineers who have a strong academic foundation, who have acquired technical knowledge and skills, and who stay up-to-date on changing technologies provide themselves with the versatility and flexibility to succeed within the electronics industry.

FOR MORE INFORMATION

For information on careers and educational programs, contact the following associations:

Institute of Electrical and Electronics Engineers
1828 L Street, NW, Suite 1202
Washington, DC 20036-5104
Tel: 202-785-0017
Email: ieeeusa@ieee.org
http://www.ieee.org

Electronic Industries Alliance
2500 Wilson Boulevard
Arlington, VA 22201-3834

Tel: 703-907-7500
http://www.eia.org

For information on the Summer at Delphi Youth Program for high school students, contact
The Delphian School
20950 SW Rock Creek Road
Sheridan, OR 97378-9740
Tel: 800-626-6610
Email: info@delphian.org
http://www.delphian.org

For information on careers, educational programs, and student clubs, contact
Junior Engineering Technical Society
1420 King Street, Suite 405
Alexandria, VA 22314-2794
Tel: 703-548-5387
Email: info@jets.org
http://www.jets.org

For information on its summer youth program for high school students, contact
Michigan Technological University Summer Youth Program
Youth Programs Office
Alumni House
1400 Townsend Drive
Houghton, MI 49931-1295
Tel: 906-487-2219
http://youthprograms.mtu.edu

=========== **INTERVIEW** ===========

Timothy D. Swieter is an electrical engineer for Birket Engineering, Inc., an entertainment engineering company in Orlando, Florida. He discussed his career with the editors of Careers in Focus: Engineering.

Q. Why did you decide to become an electrical engineer?
A. I knew I wanted to work in the entertainment industry. I knew that I had a knack for taking things apart and trying to understand them. As a kid I played with LEGOs and Constructs nonstop. Over time my opinion was formed

that engineering fit what I wanted to do. During high school I studied any materials I could find about the entertainment industry. I was fascinated with the technical articles and the TV shows showing the behind-the-scenes and how they built an attraction or accomplished some amazing engineering feat. All of these elements helped to form my desire to be an engineer.

Q. Tell us about your education and how you entered the field.

A. I attended Kettering University for my undergraduate degree in electrical engineering. Kettering's unique characteristic is that it is a co-op school. Every student has to find employment in a field related to their career. I worked for Rapistan Systems, which engineered and built material handling equipment for airports, distribution centers, and postal facilities. The schedule at Kettering was such that I attended school for three months and then I worked for Rapistan Systems for three months. This repeated for my entire career at Kettering. I think that co-op is a must for all careers—especially engineering! Learning theory is not enough; practicing it in the real world is a tremendous advantage to getting ahead and understanding what a real engineer is.

When I started my last term at school the economy was bad and our company was just bought by Siemens. During my first week of my last term at school I was told by Rapistan that they could not hire me because of complications with the layoffs that were occurring.

Knowing that I did not have a job after my last term of school ended, I continued contacting companies in the entertainment business. I had some dialog with one company, Birket Engineering Inc., for several months prior to my bad news from Rapistan. I would trade an e-mail every now and then to let Glenn Birket (the president) know how things were going at school and at work. In one of my e-mails I mentioned that I was going to be jobless by the end of the summer. In September, he offered to fly me down to Orlando to meet me for an interview.

A couple days after the interview, Birket Engineering offered me a job as an electrical engineer doing ride and show control safety systems. I started working for BEI on October 6, 2003—my dream job. Within a week of completing school I was writing software for controlling the next major attraction at Universal Orlando.

Q. Tell us about your work at Birket Engineering. What are your tasks/responsibilities on a typical day or for a typical project?

A. Birket Engineering Inc. creates control system for rides and shows. We are known for doing the life safety aspects of a system. We are system integrators taking products made by various manufacturers and applying them in a fail-safe method to perform a desired response or action. It may be using linear induction motors to launch a roller coaster or brakes to stop the same coaster or pyrotechnic controllers for fireworks or a system that synchronizes the audio, video, and show equipment together during a performance. I have worked on the ride control system for Revenge of the Mummy at Universal Orlando and Universal Hollywood, the control system for the nighttime fireworks show at Hong Kong Disneyland, and the show control system for Fear Factor Live! at Universal Studios Hollywood. Overall, it is my responsibility to meet the customer's requirement and to ensure that it is done in a safe manner.

Because we are a small company I am able to be more than just an engineer—which is a good thing. I am able to wear many hats, including marketing, bidding on new projects, and meeting with potential clients or sub-vendors. At times I may work 30- or 40-hour weeks, other times I may work 80- to 100-hour weeks. Although there is no one typical day, let me try and explain the life of a project:

A project life:
Our client will usually come to us with an idea for a new ride or show. We review their ideas and provide a bid for performing the work. If we win the bid, we sign a contract and get to work. During the beginning of a project, meetings are held with the client and with other vendors. We discuss the scope of work to be accomplished and brainstorm about the various ways to approach the technical problems. Each project has its own unique requirements. We spend time researching new technology or products that will help us to tackle the design challenges.

As the design progresses the office work is comprised of creating the design and documenting it. This involves writing theory of operations, doing calculations, creating design drawings, and building prototypes. The design usually goes through a couple revisions—each time with the client—to ensure that the system still meets their needs. There can be artistic changes along the way, budget cuts/additions that change how our system works, safety issues raised, or operation and maintenance requirements. Because an attraction requires the work of many vendors oftentimes when one vendor changes a design, we too will have to adjust our hardware or software interfaces.

After the design is approved it is time for manufacturing. This is when software is written and tested and the actual system parts are bought and assembled. Sometimes this process can go smoothly; other times new problems in the design can be found and adjustments must be made.

Next is the installation phase. This involves directing work at the site to ensure the equipment is installed correctly and the proper power and cabling is present. Overlapping with the install phase is the test and adjust phase. This phase is where the hard work and dedication comes in. Test and adjust means that the equipment is powered on for the first time with all of the components together from the various vendors. The systems are tested for both functionality and safety. Again during this phase new design or safety issues will be found. To ensure that these problems are not a show stopper, we must be quick to assess the problem and develop a solution. There have been a couple times where I have worked more than 24 hours in a row to ensure that the project was done on time for a grand opening—you never want to miss a grand opening.

Q. What advice would you give to high school students who are interested in this career?

A. High school students should focus on having good learning skills, reading everything they can, and practicing their communication skills (both written and oral). Engineering is about communicating ideas, thoughts, and designs in an efficient manner so that others can understand them to produce the design. Engineering is also about analytical thinking—solving problems and thinking through the issues involved and documenting your decisions.

I would encourage high school students to get involved in science or math clubs. Don't only take physics and English classes, but take an art class, a technical drawing class, or a shop class. Volunteer in the theater or find a robotics club. FIRST is a popular robotics club for high school students. Do activities that challenge you, and find people who will help you explore your interests. When you get to college, continue this trend. Yes, academics are important, but so is what you do outside the classroom. Are you a lifelong learner? Do you have hobbies that you like to pursue? I did all of the above activities, and they helped me to explore what I liked and disliked. They also helped me to find what I was good at and what I wasn't.

Q. What are the three most important professional qualities for electrical engineers?

A. The professional qualities that I think are important for an electrical engineer are not necessarily industry-wide thinking. Many of the qualities that I think are important go to the core of the person and are not something that one picks up in a classroom. These include integrity, self motivation, and being humble.

Integrity. As an entertainment engineering company, we have a great responsibility to both our client and the guest's safety while experiencing the attraction. No matter the size of the corporation or the circumstance, truth will prevail and doing the right thing is important. As an engineer you have the obligation to better society through the application of math and science; this responsibility should not be taken lightly.

Motivation/self-directing. No one tells me what to do each day when I come to work. I think in any job it is important to be of a mind-set that is willing and eager for work. Engineering is about solving problems, designing and working through solutions. We have to find the answers; therefore we have to be motivated to go looking for them.

Being humble. When working through a problem, you will often receive many opinions from coworkers or need to brush up on the theory you learned in school. Take time to relearn what you learned in college or to explore the advice provided by others. Being humble to search for answers, ask for help, and critically evaluate your work is good. To be good at engineering requires experience; this is one profession where they don't teach you everything in college.

Engineering Technicians

OVERVIEW

Engineering technicians use engineering, science, and mathematics to help engineers and other professionals in research and development, quality control, manufacturing, and many other fields. Approximately 532,000 engineering technicians are employed in the United States.

HISTORY

Engineering technicians assist engineers, scientists, and other workers in a variety of tasks. They are highly trained workers with strong backgrounds in a specialized technological field, such as aerospace, civil, materials, and many other types of engineering. In short, engineering technicians can be found supporting engineers and other workers in any engineering discipline that comes to mind. They bridge the gap between the engineers who design the products, structures, and machines, and those who implement them. Engineering technicians have been valuable members of the engineering team ever since the first engineering projects were envisioned, planned, and implemented.

THE JOB

You may not know it, but engineering technicians play a role in almost every part of our daily lives. We can thank engineering technicians (along with engineers, scientists, and other workers)

An engineering technician (foreground) gathers apples exiting a flatbed brush washer within a containment chamber in a biosafety pilot plant. *(Agricultural Research Service)*

for safer cars and planes, drugs that work effectively when we are sick, well-constructed buildings and highways, clean water and air, and the computer games we play for hours, among many other things that we take for granted.

Some of the major technician specialties include electrical and electronics engineering, civil engineering, industrial engineering, and mechanical engineering. The following paragraphs provide more information on these and other engineering technician specialties:

Aeronautical and aerospace engineering technicians design, construct, test, operate, and maintain the basic structures of aircraft and spacecraft, as well as propulsion and control systems. They work with scientists and aeronautical aerospace engineers. Many aeronautical and aerospace engineering technicians assist engineers in preparing equipment drawings, diagrams, blueprints, and scale models. They collect information, make computations, and perform laboratory tests.

Biomedical engineering technicians use engineering and life science principles to help biomedical engineers and scientists research biological aspects of animal and human life. They help design and construct health care instruments and devices and apply engineering principles to the study of human systems.

Chemical engineering technicians assist chemists and chemical engineers in the research, development, testing, and manufacturing of chemicals and chemical-based products.

Civil engineering technicians help civil engineers design, plan, and build public as well as private works to meet the community's needs. Civil engineers and technicians work together for the community, providing better, faster transportation; designing and developing highways, airports, and railroads; improving the environment; and constructing buildings, bridges, and space platforms. These engineering professionals work in one of the seven main civil engineering areas: structural, geotechnical, environmental, water resources, transportation, construction, and urban and community planning. The work is closely related, so a technician might work in one, or many, of these areas. A variety of subspecialties are available, including structural engineering technicians, geotechnical engineering technicians, materials technicians, urban and community planning technicians, research engineering technicians, sales engineering, transportation technicians, highway technicians, rail and waterway technicians, and construction engineering technicians.

Electrical and electronics engineering technicians work individually or with engineers to help design, produce, improve, maintain, test, and repair a wide range of electronic equipment. Equipment varies from consumer goods like televisions, computers, and home entertainment components, to industrial, military, and medical goods, such as radar and laser equipment. Electronic devices play a part in practically every business and even many leisure activities found around the globe. Such diverse activities as NASA space missions, sophisticated medical testing procedures, and car and airplane travel would be impossible without the use of electronic equipment. The products made by the electronics industry can be divided into four basic categories: government products (which include missile and space guidance systems, communications systems, medical technology, and traffic control devices), industrial products (which include large-scale computers, radio and television broadcasting equipment, telecommunications equipment, and electronic office equipment), consumer products (which includes televisions, DVD players, and radios), and components (which comprises the smaller pieces that make up all electronics, such as capacitors, switches, transistors, relays, and amplifiers). Subspecialties in this career field include electronics development technicians, electronics drafters, cost-estimating technicians, electronics manufacturing and production technicians, and electronics service and maintenance technicians.

Environmental engineering technicians help environmental engineers and scientists design, build, and maintain systems to control waste streams produced by municipalities or private industry. Environmental engineering technicians typically focus on one of three areas: air, land, or water.

Industrial engineering technicians assist industrial engineers in their duties: they collect and analyze data and make recommendations for the efficient use of personnel, materials, and machines to produce goods or to provide services. They may study the time, movements, and methods a worker uses to accomplish daily tasks in production, maintenance, or clerical areas. The kind of work done by industrial engineering technicians varies, depending on the size and type of company for which they work. A variety of subspecialties are available, including methods engineering technicians, materials handling technicians, plant layout technicians, work measurement technicians, time-study technicians, production-control technicians, and inventory control technicians.

Materials engineering technicians work in support of materials engineers and scientists. These jobs involve the production, quality control, and experimental study of metals, ceramics, glass, plastics, semiconductors, and composites (combinations of these materials). Metallurgical technicians may conduct tests on the properties of the aforementioned materials, develop and modify test procedures and equipment, analyze data, and prepare reports.

Mechanical engineering technicians work under the direction of mechanical engineers to design, build, maintain, and modify many kinds of machines, mechanical devices, and tools. They work in a wide range of industries and in a variety of specific jobs within every industry. Technicians may specialize in any one of many areas, including biomedical equipment, measurement and control, products manufacturing, solar energy, turbo machinery, energy resource technology, and engineering materials and technology.

Petroleum engineering technicians help petroleum engineers and scientists improve petroleum drilling technology, maximize field production, and provide technical assistance.

Robotics technicians assist robotics engineers in a wide variety of tasks relating to the design, development, production, testing, operation, repair, and maintenance of robots and robotic devices.

Engineering technicians work in a variety of conditions depending on their field of specialization. Technicians who specialize in design may find that they spend most of their time at the drafting board or computer. Those who specialize in manufacturing may spend some time at a desk but also spend considerable time in manufacturing areas or shops.

Conditions also vary according to industry. Some industries require technicians to work in foundries, die-casting rooms, machine shops, assembly areas, or punch-press areas. Most of these areas, however, are well lighted, heated, and ventilated. Moreover, most industries employing mechanical engineering technicians have strong safety programs.

REQUIREMENTS

High School

Preparation for this career begins in high school. Although entrance requirements to associate programs vary somewhat from school to school, mathematics and physical science form the backbone of a good preparatory curriculum. Classes should include algebra, geometry, science, trigonometry, calculus, chemistry, mechanical drawing, shop, and physics. Because computers have become essential for engineering technicians, computer courses are also important.

English and speech courses provide invaluable experience in improving verbal and written communication skills. Since some technicians go on to become technical writers or teachers, and since all of them need to be able to explain technical matter clearly and concisely, communication skills are important.

Postsecondary Training

While some current engineering technicians enter the field without formal academic training, it is increasingly difficult to do so. Most employers are interested in hiring graduates with at least a two-year degree in engineering technology. Technical institutes, community colleges, vocational schools, and universities all offer this course of study.

The Technology Accreditation Commission of the Accreditation Board for Engineering and Technology (http://www.abet.org) accredits engineering technology programs.

Some engineering technicians decide to pursue advancement in their field by becoming engineer technologists. Others decide to branch off into research and development or become engineers. These higher-level and higher-paid positions typically require the completion of a bachelor's degree in engineering technology (for engineering technologists) or at least a bachelor's degree in engineering (for technicians interested in research and development and engineers).

Certification or Licensing

Certification and licensing requirements vary by specialty. Check with your state's department of labor and professional associations within your field for further information.

Many engineering technicians choose to become certified by the National Institute for Certification in Engineering Technologies. To become certified, you must combine a specific amount of job-related experience with a written examination. Certifications are offered at several levels of expertise. Such certification is generally voluntary, although obtaining certification shows a high level of commitment and dedication that employers find highly desirable.

Electronics engineering technicians may obtain voluntary certification from the International Society of Certified Electronics Technicians and the Electronics Technicians Association, International. This certification is regarded as a demonstration of professional dedication, determination, and know-how.

Engineering technicians are encouraged to become affiliated with professional groups, such as the American Society of Certified Engineering Technicians (ASCET), that offer continuing education sessions for members. Additionally, some engineering technicians may be required to belong to unions.

Other Requirements

All engineering technicians are relied upon for solutions and must express their ideas clearly in speech and in writing. Good communication skills are important for a technician in the writing and presenting of reports and plans. These skills are also important for working alongside other technicians and professionals, people who are often from many different backgrounds and skilled in varying areas of engineering.

Engineering technicians need mathematical and mechanical aptitude. They must understand abstract concepts and apply scientific principles to problems in the shop, laboratory, or work site.

Many tasks assigned to engineering technicians require patience and methodical, persistent work. Good technicians work well with their hands, paying close attention to every detail of a project. Some technicians are bored by the repetitiveness of some tasks, while others enjoy the routine.

Individuals planning to advance beyond the technician's level should be willing to and capable of pursuing some form of higher education.

EXPLORING

If you are interested in a career as an engineering technician, you can gain relevant experience by taking shop courses, joining electronics or radio clubs in school, and assembling electronic equipment with commercial kits.

You should take every opportunity to discuss the field with people working in it. Try to visit a variety of different kinds of engineering facilities—service shops, manufacturing plants, and research laboratories—either through individual visits or through field trips organized by teachers or guidance counselors. These visits will provide a realistic idea of the opportunities in the different areas of the industry. If you enroll in a community college or technical school, you may be able to secure off-quarter or part-time internships with local employers through your school's career services office. Internships are valuable ways to gain experience while still in school.

EMPLOYERS

Approximately 532,000 engineering technicians are employed in the United States. About 36 percent of all technicians work in manufacturing and 22 percent work in professional, scientific, and technical service industries.

STARTING OUT

Most technical schools, community colleges, and universities have career services offices. Companies actively recruit employees while they are still in school or are nearing graduation. Because these job services are the primary source of entry-level jobs for engineering technicians, you should check out a school's placement rate for your specific field before making a final decision about which school you attend.

Another way to obtain employment is through direct contact with a particular company. It is best to write to the personnel department and include a resume summarizing your education and experience. If the company has an appropriate opening, a company representative will schedule an interview with you. There are also many excellent public and commercial employment organizations that can help graduates obtain jobs appropriate to their training and experience.

Newspaper want ads and employment services are other methods of getting jobs. Professional or trade magazines often have job listings and can be good sources for job seekers. Professional associations compile information on job openings and publish job lists. For example, the International Society of Certified Electronics Technicians offers lists of job openings around the country at its Web site. Information about job openings can also be found in trade magazines. Professional organizations are also good for networking with other technicians and are up to date on industry advancement, changes, and areas of employment.

ADVANCEMENT

As engineering technicians remain with a company, they become more valuable to the employer. Opportunities for advancement are available for engineering technicians who are willing to accept greater responsibilities either by specializing in a specific field, taking on more technically complex assignments, or by assuming supervisory duties. Some technicians advance by moving into technical sales or customer relations. Others pursue advanced education to become engineering technologists or engineers.

EARNINGS

The earnings of engineering technicians vary widely depending on skills and experience, the type of work, geographical location, and other factors. The U.S. Department of Labor reports the following mean earnings for engineering technicians by specialty in 2005: aerospace engineering, $52,720; civil engineering, $40,780; electrical and electronic engineering, $48,710; environmental engineering, $41,940; industrial engineering, $49,220; and mechanical engineering, $46,520. Salaries ranged from less than $24,500 to $76,620 or more annually.

Engineering technicians generally receive premium pay for overtime work on Sundays and holidays and for evening and night shift work. Most employers offer benefits packages that include paid holidays, paid vacations, sick days, and health insurance. Companies may also offer pension and retirement plans, profit sharing, 401(k) plans, tuition assistance programs, and release time for additional education.

WORK ENVIRONMENT

Depending on their jobs, engineering technicians may work in the shop or office areas or in both. The type of plant facilities depends on the product. For example, an electronics plant producing small electronic products requiring very exacting tolerances has very clean working conditions. Other engineering technicians, such as those in civil engineering, may work outdoors.

Engineering technicians often travel to other locations or areas. They may accompany engineers to technical conventions or on visits to other companies to gain insight into new or different methods of operation and production.

Continuing education plays a large role in the life of engineering technicians. They may attend classes or seminars, keeping up-to-date with emerging technology and methods of managing production efficiently.

Hours of work may vary and depend on factory shifts. Engineering technicians are often asked to get jobs done quickly and to meet very tight deadlines.

OUTLOOK

According to the *Occupational Outlook Handbook,* employment of engineering technicians is expected to increase about as fast as the average for all occupations through 2014. Computer-aided design allows individual technicians to increase productivity, thereby limiting job growth. Those with training in sophisticated technologies and those with degrees in technology will have the best employment opportunities. Faster-than-average employment growth is predicted for environmental engineering technicians as a result of increasing focus on the protection of the environment.

FOR MORE INFORMATION

Visit the ASEE's precollege Web site for information on engineering and engineering technology careers.

American Society for Engineering Education (ASEE)
1818 N Street, NW, Suite 600
Washington, DC 20036-2479
Tel: 202-331-3500
http://www.engineeringk12.org/students/default.htm

Contact the society for information on training and certification.

American Society of Certified Engineering
    Technicians
PO Box 1536
Brandon, MS 39043-1536
Tel: 601-824-8991
Email: general-manager@ascet.org
http://www.ascet.org

This organization offers information on certification and student membership.
Electronics Technicians Association International
Five Depot Street
Greencastle, IN 46135-8024
Tel: 800-288-3824
Email: eta@eta-i.org
http://www.eta-sda.com

Contact the society for information on certification and student membership.
International Society of Certified Electronics Technicians
3608 Pershing Avenue
Fort Worth, TX 76107-4527
Tel: 817-921-9101
Email: info@iscet.org
http://www.iscet.org

For information on careers, educational programs, and student clubs, contact
Junior Engineering Technical Society
1420 King Street, Suite 405
Alexandria, VA 22314-2794
Tel: 703-548-5387
Email: info@jets.org
http://www.jets.org

Environmental Engineers

OVERVIEW

Environmental engineers design, build, and maintain systems to control waste streams produced by municipalities or private industry. Such waste streams may be wastewater, solid waste, hazardous waste, or contaminated emissions to the atmosphere (air pollution). Environmental engineers typically are employed by the Environmental Protection Agency (EPA), by private industry, or by engineering consulting firms. There are about 49,000 environmental engineers employed in the United States.

HISTORY

Although people have been doing work that falls into the category of environmental engineering for decades, it is only within about the last 30 years that a separate professional category has been recognized for environmental engineers.

Post-Civil War industrialization and urbanization created life-threatening water and air quality problems. These problems continued during and after World War II, dramatically increasing all forms of environmental pollution. After the war, pollution control technologies were developed to deal with the damage.

"In the 1930s, 1940s, 1950s, even the 1960s, someone who wanted to be an environmental engineer would have been steered toward sanitary engineering, which basically deals with things like wastewater, putting sewers down," says Lee DeAngelis, regional director of the Environmental Careers Organization (ECO).

Interesting Web Sites

All Engineering Schools
http://www.allengineeringschools.com

ASEE Engineering K12 Center
http://www.engineeringk12.org

Engineer Girl!
http://www.engineergirl.org

A Sightseer's Guide to Engineering
http://www.engineeringsights.org

Yahoo: Engineering
http://dir.yahoo.com/science/engineering

Sanitary engineering is a form of civil engineering. "Civil engineering is engineering for municipalities," explains Mike Waxman, who heads the environmental training arm of the outreach department at the University of Wisconsin-Madison College of Engineering. "It includes things like building roads, highways, buildings. But a big part of civil engineering is dealing with the waste streams that come from cities or municipalities. Wastewater from a city's sewage treatment plants is a prime example," Waxman says. This water must be treated in order to be pure enough to be used again. "Scientists work out what must be done to break down the harmful substances in the water, such as by adding bacteria; engineers design, build, and maintain the systems needed to carry this out. Technicians monitor the systems, take samples, run tests, and otherwise ensure that the system is working as it should."

This structure—scientists deciding what should be done at the molecular or biological level, engineers designing the systems needed to carry out the project, and technicians taking care of the day-to-day monitoring of the systems—is applied to other waste streams as well, Waxman adds.

Environmental engineering is an offshoot of civil engineering/ sanitary engineering and focuses on the development of the physical systems needed to control waste streams. Civil engineers who already were doing this type of work began to refer to themselves as environmental engineers around 1970 with the great boom in new environmental regulations, according to Waxman. "It's what they wanted to be called," he says. "They wanted the recognition for what they were doing."

THE JOB

There is a small pond in Crawford County, Illinois, which provides the habitat and primary food source for several different species of fish, frogs, turtles, insects, and birds, as well as small mammals. About a half-mile away is the Jack J. Ryan and Sons Manufacturing Company. For years, this plant has safely treated its wastewater—produced during the manufacturing process—and discharged it into the pond. Then one day, without warning, hundreds of dead fish wash up on the banks of the pond. What's going on? What should be done? It is the job of environmental engineers to investigate and design a system to make the water safe for the flora and fauna that depend on it for survival.

Environmental engineers who work for the federal or state Environmental Protection Agency (EPA) act as police officers or detectives. They investigate problems stemming from systems that aren't functioning properly. They have knowledge about wastewater treatment systems and have the authority to enforce environmental regulations.

The Crawford County pond is in the jurisdiction of the Champaign regional office of the Illinois Environmental Protection Agency (IEPA). There are three divisions: air, land, and water. An environmental engineer in the water division would be alerted to the fish kill at the pond and head out to the site to investigate. The engineer takes photographs and samples of the water and makes notes to document the problem. He or she considers the possibilities: Is it a discharge problem from Jack J. Ryan and Sons? If so, was there an upset in the process? A spill? A flood? Could a storage tank be leaking? Or is the problem further upstream? The pond is connected to other waterways, so could some other discharger be responsible for killing the fish?

The engineer visits Jack J. Ryan and Sons to talk to the production manager and ask if the plant has been doing anything differently lately. The investigation might include a tour of the plant or an examination of its plans. It might also include questioning other manufacturers further upstream, to see if they are doing something new that's caused the fish kill.

Once the problem has been identified, the environmental engineer and the plant officials can work together on the solution. For example, the production manager at Jack J. Ryan and Sons reports that they've changed something in the manufacturing process to produce a new kind of die-cast part. They didn't know they were doing something wrong. The EPA engineer informs the company they'll be fined $10,000, and a follow-up investigation will be conducted to make sure it has complied with regulations.

Jack J. Ryan and Sons may have its own environmental engineer on staff. This engineer's job is to help keep the company in compliance with federal and state regulations while balancing the economic concerns of the company. At one time, industries' environmental affairs positions were often filled by employees who also had other positions in the plant. Since the late 1980s, however, these positions are held by environmental experts, including scientists, engineers, lawyers, and communications professionals.

In the Crawford County pond scenario, a Ryan and Sons environmental expert might get a call from an engineer at the IEPA: "There seems to be a fish kill at the pond near your plant. We've determined it's probably from a discharge from your plant." The Ryan and Sons expert looks at the plant's plans, talks to the production manager, and figures out a plan of action to bring the company into compliance.

Some companies rely on environmental engineering consulting firms instead of keeping an engineer on staff. Consulting firms usually provide teams that visit the plant, assess the problem, and design a system to get the plant back into compliance. Consulting firms not only know the technical aspects of waste control, but also have expertise in dealing with the government—filling out the required government forms, for example.

Broadly speaking, environmental engineers may focus on one of three areas: air, land, or water. Those who are concerned with air work on air pollution control, air quality management, and other specialties involved in systems to treat emissions. The private sector tends to have the majority of these jobs, according to the Environmental Careers Organization. Environmental engineers focused on land include landfill professionals, for whom environmental engineering and public health are key areas. Engineers focused on water work on activities similar to those described above.

A big area for environmental engineers is hazardous waste management. Expertise in designing systems and processes to reduce, recycle, and treat hazardous waste streams is very much in demand, according to the ECO. This area tends to be the most technical of all the environmental fields and so demands more professionals with graduate and technical degrees.

Environmental engineers spend a lot of time on paperwork—including writing reports and memos and filling out forms. They also might climb a smokestack, wade in a creek, or go toe-to-toe with a district attorney in a battle over a compliance matter. If they work on company staffs, they may face frustration over not knowing what is going on in their own plants. If they work for the government, they might struggle with bureaucracy. If they work for a consultant, they may have to juggle the needs of the client (including the need to keep costs down) with the demands of the government.

REQUIREMENTS

High School

A bachelor's degree is mandatory to work in environmental engineering. At the high school level, the most important course work is in science and mathematics. It's also good to develop written communication skills. Competition to get into the top engineering schools is tough, so it's important to do well on your ACT or SAT tests.

Postsecondary Training

About 20 schools offer an undergraduate degree in environmental engineering. Another possibility is to earn a civil engineering, mechanical engineering, industrial engineering, or other traditional engineering degree with an environmental focus. You could also obtain a traditional engineering degree and learn the environmental knowledge on the job, or obtain a master's degree in environmental engineering.

Certification or Licensing

If your work as an engineer affects public health, safety, or property, you must register with the state. To obtain registration, you must have a degree from an accredited engineering program. Right before you get your degree (or soon after), you must pass an Engineer-in-Training (EIT) exam covering fundamentals of science and engineering. A few years after you've started your career, you also must pass an exam covering engineering practice. For more information on licensing and examination requirements, visit http://www.ncees.org. Additional certification is voluntary and may be obtained through such organizations as the American Academy of Environmental Engineers.

Other Requirements

Environmental engineers must like solving problems and have a good background in science and math. They must be able to, in the words of one engineer, "just get in there and figure out what needs to be done." Engineers must be able to communicate verbally and in writing with a variety of people from both technical and nontechnical backgrounds.

EXPLORING

A good way to explore becoming an environmental engineer is to talk to someone in the field. Contact your local EPA office, check the Yellow Pages for environmental consulting firms in your area, or ask a local industrial company if you can visit. The latter is not as far-fetched as you might think: Big industry has learned the value of earning positive community relations, and their outreach efforts may include having an open house for their neighbors in which one can walk through their plants, ask questions, and get a feel for what goes on there.

You cannot practice at being an environmental engineer without having a bachelor's degree. However, you can put yourself in situations in which you're around environmental engineers to see what they do and how they work. To do so, you may volunteer for the local chapter of a nonprofit environmental organization, do an internship through ECO or another organization, or work first as an environmental technician, a job that requires less education (such as a two-year associate's degree or even a high school diploma).

Another good way to get exposure to environmental engineering is to familiarize yourself with professional journals. Two journals that may be available in your library include *Chemical & Engineering News,* which regularly features articles on waste management systems, and *Pollution Engineering,* which features articles of interest to environmental engineers.

EMPLOYERS

Approximately 49,000 environmental engineers are employed in the United States. Environmental engineers most often work for the Environmental Protection Agency (EPA), in private industry, or at engineering consulting firms.

STARTING OUT

The traditional method of entering this field is by obtaining a bachelor's degree and applying directly to companies or to the EPA. School career services offices can assist you in these efforts.

ADVANCEMENT

After environmental engineers have gained work experience, there are several routes for advancement. Those working for the EPA can become a department supervisor or switch to private industry or consulting. In-house environmental staff members may rise to supervisory positions. Engineers with consulting firms may become project managers or specialists in certain areas.

Environmental careers are evolving at a breakneck speed. New specialties are emerging all the time. Advancement may take the form of getting involved at the beginning stages of a new subspecialty that suits an engineer's particular interests, experience, and expertise.

EARNINGS

The U.S. Department of Labor reports that mean annual earnings of environmental engineers were $70,720 in 2005. Salaries for environmental engineers ranged from less than $42,570 for the lowest paid 10 percent to more than $104,610 for the highest paid 10 percent. According to a 2005 salary survey by the National Association of Colleges and Employers, bachelor's degree candidates in environmental/environmental health received starting offers averaging $47,384 a year.

According to the American Academy of Environmental Engineers, engineers with a bachelor of science degree were receiving starting salaries ranging from $36,000 to $42,000 with some as much as $48,000 in the late 1990s. Those with a master's degree earned $40,000 to $45,000 and those with a Ph.D. earned $42,000 to $50,000. Licensed engineers with five years of experience can expect to earn from $50,000 to $60,000.

Fringe benefits vary widely depending on the employer. State EPA jobs may include, for example, two weeks of vacation, health insurance, tuition reimbursement, use of company vehicles for work, and similar perks. In-house or consulting positions may add additional benefits to lure top candidates.

WORK ENVIRONMENT

Environmental engineers split their time between working in an office and working out in the field. They may also spend time in courtrooms. Since ongoing education is crucial in most of these positions, engineers must attend training sessions and workshops and study new regulations, techniques, and problems. They usually work as part of a team that may include any of a number of different specialists. Engineers must also give presentations of technical information to those with both technical and nontechnical backgrounds.

OUTLOOK

The *Occupational Outlook Handbook* projects that employment for environmental engineers will grow much faster than the average for all occupations through 2014. Engineers will be needed to clean up existing hazards and help companies comply with government regulations. The shift toward prevention of problems and protecting public health should create job opportunities.

Jobs are available with all three major employers—the EPA, industry, and consulting firms. The EPA has long been a big employer of environmental engineers.

FOR MORE INFORMATION

For information on certification, careers, and salaries or a copy of Environmental Engineering Selection Guide *(giving names of accredited environmental engineering programs and of professors who have board certification as environmental engineers), contact*

American Academy of Environmental Engineers
130 Holiday Court, Suite 100
Annapolis, MD 21401-7003
Tel: 410-266-3311
Email: info@aaee.net
http://www.aaee.net

For information on internships and career guidance, contact
Environmental Careers Organization
30 Winter Street, 6th Floor
Boston, MA 02108-4720
Tel: 617-426-4783
http://www.eco.org

For career guidance information, contact
Junior Engineering Technical Society Inc.
1420 King Street, Suite 405
Alexandria, VA 22314-2794
Tel: 703-548-5387
Email: info@jets.org
http://www.jets.org

The following is a cross-disciplinary environmental association.
National Association of Environmental Professionals
389 Main Street, Suite 202
Malden, MA 02148-5017
Tel: 888-251-9902
Email: office@naep.org
http://www.naep.org

For information about the private waste services industry, contact
National Solid Wastes Management Association
4301 Connecticut Avenue, NW, Suite 300
Washington, DC 20008-2304
Tel: 202-244-4700
http://www.nswma.org

Contact the SCA for information about internships for high school students.
Student Conservation Association (SCA)
689 River Road
PO Box 550
Charlestown, NH 03603-0550
Tel: 603-543-1700
http://www.sca-inc.org

Hardware Engineers

QUICK FACTS

School Subjects
Computer science
Mathematics

Personal Skills
Mechanical/manipulative
Technical/scientific

Work Environment
Primarily indoors
Primarily one location

Minimum Education Level
Bachelor's degree

Salary Range
$52,464 to $84,420 to
$128,300+

Certification or Licensing
Voluntary

Outlook
About as fast as the average

DOT
030

GOE
02.07.01

NOC
2147

O*NET-SOC
17-2061.00

OVERVIEW

Computer *hardware engineers* design, build, and test computer hardware (such as computer chips and circuit boards) and computer systems. They also work with peripheral devices such as printers, scanners, modems, and monitors, among others. Hardware engineers are employed by a variety of companies, some of which specialize in business, accounting, science, or engineering. Most hardware engineers have a degree in computer science or engineering or equivalent computer background. There are approximately 78,500 computer hardware engineers employed in the United States.

HISTORY

What started as a specialty of electrical engineering has developed into a career field of its own. Today, many individuals interested in a career in one of the computer industry's most promising sectors turn to computer engineering. Computer engineers improve, repair, and implement changes needed to keep up with the demand for faster and stronger computers and complex software programs. Some specialize in the design of the hardware: computer or peripheral parts such as memory chips, motherboards, or microprocessors. Others specialize in creating and organizing information systems for businesses and the government.

More and more businesses rely on computers for information networking, accessing the Internet, and data processing for their daily activities. Also, computers are now affordable, allowing many families to purchase systems. Peripherals, such as printers, scanners, and disk drives, are popular accessories available to complete a variety of tasks. Computer engineers are also needed to develop and improve technology needed for consumer products, such as cellular phones, microwave ovens, compact disc players, digital video disc players, high-definition televisions, and video games. Engineers turn to program tools, such as computer-aided design (CAD), to help them create new products. CAD programs are often used with computer-aided manufacturing (CAM) programs to produce three-dimensional drawings that can be easily altered or manipulated, and direct the actual production of hardware components.

THE JOB

Computer hardware engineers work with the physical parts of computers, such as CPUs (computer processing units), motherboards, chipsets, video cards, cooling units, magnetic tape, disk drives, storage devices, network cards, and all the components that connect them, down to wires, nuts, and bolts.

Hardware engineers design parts and create prototypes to test, using CAD/CAM technology to make schematic drawings. They assemble the parts using fine hand tools, soldering irons, and microscopes. Parts are reworked and developed through multiple testing procedures. Once a final design is completed, hardware engineers oversee the manufacture and installation of parts.

Computer hardware engineers also work on peripherals, such as keyboards, printers, monitors, mice, track balls, modems, scanners, external storage devices, speaker systems, and digital cameras.

Some hardware engineers are involved in maintenance and repair of computers, networks, and peripherals. They troubleshoot problems, order or make new parts, and install them. Calvin Prior is a network systems administrator for TASC, a nonprofit social service agency headquartered in Chicago, Illinois. He is responsible for the day-to-day operations of a statewide network of over 300 servers. Prior starts work early; most mornings he's at his desk by 7:30 A.M. His first task of the day is making sure the network files from the previous day backed up successfully. Then he checks for e-mail and voice mail messages and promptly responds to urgent problems.

Daily meetings are held to keep informed on department business. "It's very short and informal," says Prior. "We discuss urgent business or upcoming projects and schedules." The rest of the morning is spent working on various projects, troubleshooting systems, or phone work with TASC's remote offices. After a quick lunch break and if no network breakdowns or glitches occur, Prior usually spends his afternoons researching hardware products or responding to user requests.

Since computer technology changes so rapidly, it is important to keep up with the development of new parts and the procedures for incorporating them into older systems as soon as they become available.

The workload changes daily, leaving some days more hectic than others. "It's important to be flexible," says Prior. "And be good at multitasking." If a major problem cannot be solved over the phone, Prior must travel to the source. Solutions are not always simple; some require changing hardware or redesigning the system. Prior often upgrades or reworks systems in the early morning, late at night, or on weekends to minimize the disruption of work. Major network problems require a complete shutdown of the entire system. "The fewer servers on the network, the better," he says.

Engineering professionals like Prior must be familiar with different network systems such as local area networks (LAN), wide area networks (WAN), among others, as well as programming languages suited to their company's needs. Many work as part of a team of specialists who use elements of science, math, and electronics to improve existing technology or implement solutions.

REQUIREMENTS

High School
Calvin Prior credits high school computer and electronics classes and programming courses for giving him a good head start in this career. You should also take math and physics, as well as speech and writing courses so that you will be able to communicate effectively with coworkers and clients.

Postsecondary Training
Hardware engineers need at least a bachelor's degree in computer engineering or electrical engineering. Employment in research laboratories or academic institutions might require a master's or Ph.D. in computer science or engineering. For a list of accredited four-year computer engineering programs, contact the Accreditation Board for Engineering and Technology.

College studies might include such computer science courses as computer architecture, systems design, chip design, microprocessor design, and network architecture, in addition to a heavy concentration of math and science classes.

Certification or Licensing
Not all computer professionals are certified. The deciding factor seems to be if it is required by their employer. Many companies offer

Hardware engineers troubleshoot a malfunctioning server. *(Corbis)*

tuition reimbursement, or incentives, to those who earn certification. Certification is available in a variety of specialties. The Institute for Certification of Computing Professionals, offers the associate computing professional designation for those new to the field and the certified computing professional designation for those with at least 48 months of full-time professional level work in computer-based information systems. Certification is considered by many to be a measure of industry knowledge as well as leverage when negotiating salary.

Other Requirements

Hardware engineers need a broad knowledge of and experience with computer systems and technologies. You need strong problem-solving and analysis skills and good interpersonal skills. Patience, self-motivation, and flexibility are important. Often, a number of projects are worked on simultaneously, so the ability to multitask is important. Because of rapid technological advances in the computer field, continuing education is a necessity.

EXPLORING

Ask your computer teacher or guidance counselor to set up an information interview or job shadowing experience with a hardware engineer. You can also talk to your high school computer science teacher for more information about the career. Try to learn as much as possible about computers and computer hardware. You can learn about new developments by reading trade magazines and talking to other computer users. You can also read *Crossroads: The International ACM Student Magazine* (http://www.acm.org/pubs/crossroads), a student-written publication from the Association for Computing Machinery that covers computer-related topics. Other ways to learn more about the field include joining computer clubs and surfing the Internet for information about working in this field (the Junior Engineering Technical Society offers a wealth of information on engineering careers and competitions at its Web site, http://www.jets.org).

EMPLOYERS

Approximately 78,500 computer hardware engineers are employed in the United States. Computer hardware engineers are employed in nearly every industry by small and large corporations alike. According to the *Occupational Outlook Quarterly,* approximately 43 percent of hardware engineers are employed in computer and electronic product manufacturing.

Jobs are available nationwide, though salary averages, as reported by a recent *Computerworld* survey, tend to be higher in New York City and Los Angeles. Note, however, that these cities are notorious for their high cost of living, which, in the end, may offset a higher income.

STARTING OUT

Education and solid work experience will open industry doors. Though a bachelor's degree is a minimum requirement for most corporate giants, some companies, smaller ones especially, will hire based largely on work experience and practical training. Many computer professionals employed in the computer industry for some time do not have traditional electrical engineering or computer science degrees, but rather moved up on the basis of their work record. However, if you aspire to a management position, or want to work as a teacher, then a college degree is a necessity.

Large computer companies aggressively recruit on campus armed with signing bonuses and other incentives. Employment opportunities are posted in newspaper want ads daily, with some papers devoting a separate section to computer-related positions. The Internet offers a wealth of employment information plus several sites for browsing job openings, or to post your resume. Most companies maintain a Web page where they post employment opportunities or solicit resumes.

ADVANCEMENT

Many companies hire new grads to work as junior engineers. Problem-solving skills and the ability to implement solutions is a big part of this entry-level job. With enough work experience, junior engineers can move into positions that focus on a particular area in the computer industry, such as networks or peripherals. Landing a senior-level engineering position, such as systems architect, for example, is possible after considerable work experience and study. Aspiring hardware engineers should hone their computer skills to the highest level through continuing education, certification, or even advanced graduate study. Many high-level engineers hold a master's degree or better.

Some computer professionals working on the technical side of the industry opt to switch over to the marketing side of the business. Advancement opportunities here may include positions in product management or sales.

EARNINGS

Starting salary offers in 2005 for bachelor's degree candidates in computer engineering averaged $52,464, according to a National Association of Colleges and Employers. Master's degree candidates averaged $60,354.

The U.S. Department of Labor reports that median annual earnings of computer hardware engineers were $84,420 in 2005. Salaries ranged from less than $52,470 to more than $128,300.

Job perks, besides the usual benefit package of insurance, vacation, sick time, and profit sharing, may include stock options, continuing education or training, tuition reimbursement, flexible hours, and child care or other on-site services.

WORK ENVIRONMENT

Most hardware engineers work 40- to 50-hour weeks or more depending on the project to which they are assigned. Weekend work is common with some positions. Contrary to popular perceptions, hardware engineers do not spend their workdays cooped up in their offices. Instead, they spend the majority of their time meeting, planning, and working with various staff members from different levels of management and technical expertise.

Since it takes numerous workers to take a project from start to finish, team players are in high demand.

OUTLOOK

Employment in hardware engineering will grow about as fast as the average for all occupations through 2014, according to the U.S. Department of Labor. Foreign competition and increased productivity at U.S. companies will limit opportunities for hardware engineers. Despite this prediction, opportunities are still expected to be good as the number of new graduates entering the field will match the number of engineers leaving the field.

FOR MORE INFORMATION

For a list of accredited programs in computer engineering, contact
Accreditation Board for Engineering and Technology
111 Market Place, Suite 1050
Baltimore, MD 21202-7116
Tel: 410-347-7700
http://www.abet.org

For information regarding the computer industry, career opportunities as a computer engineer, or the association's membership requirements, contact
Association for Computing Machinery
Two Penn Plaza, Suite 701
New York, NY 10121-0701
Tel: 800-342-6626
Email: acmhelp@acm.org
http://www.acm.org

For information on a career in computer engineering and computer scholarships, contact
IEEE Computer Society
1730 Massachusetts Avenue, NW
Washington, DC 20036-1992
Tel: 202-371-0101
http://www.computer.org

For information on certification, contact
Institute for Certification of Computing Professionals
2350 East Devon Avenue, Suite 115
Des Plaines, IL 60018-4610
Tel: 800-843-8227
Email: office@iccp.org
http://www.iccp.org

For employment information, links to online career sites for computer professionals, information on membership for college students, and background on the industry, contact
Institute of Electrical and Electronics Engineers
Three Park Avenue, 17th Floor
New York, NY 10016-5997
Tel: 212-419-7900
Email: member-services@ieee.org
http://www.ieee.org

For comprehensive information about careers in electrical engineering and computer science, visit
Sloan Career Cornerstone Center
http://careercornerstone.org

━━━━━━━━━━━━━━━ **INTERVIEW** ━━━━━━━━━━━━━━━

Reena Singhal is a computer engineer at a major computer technology manufacturing company. She discussed her career with the editors of Careers in Focus: Engineering.

Q. Why did you decide to become a computer engineer?

A. Engineering is a great profession for those who like to help people with everyday problems. During my freshman year in college as an engineering major, I had a chance to explore several areas of engineering. One of the classes was Introduction to Computer Engineering. In this class, we had the opportunity to build a small robot throughout the course of the semester, working in pairs. The robot was programmable to teach the robot to move forward, backward, or side-to-side. We built the robot from scratch, soldering the circuit board together and programming directions for the robot to traverse a maze. On the last day of class, each pair sent their robot through the maze, and the teams which completed this task successfully won a prize. Robots are used in a variety of ways in the real-world today, from medical procedures to manufacturing to space exploration; this class gave me the stepping stone to finally see how math and science could be applied to an actual working product on a small scale.

Q. Tell us about your daily job duties as a computer engineer.

A. I am currently working on a team that is designing a next-generation microprocessor, or computer chip. This chip, like the one found in a desktop or laptop, is the "brain" of the computer, controlling its primary functionality. The chip is very complex in order to run a variety of applications, such as Internet browsers, video games, word processors and spreadsheets, and e-mail programs. I currently focus on the performance of the chip, aiming to make the next-generation computer as fast and efficient as possible, so that a user will be happy with the computer performance when using it for tasks as I mentioned above.

When focusing on performance, we look at a variety of applications that we think would be used heavily in the future on a new processor, such as games, multimedia displays, complex arithmetic, music playback, search engines, and animation. We need to speculate how computers will be used in three or four years, because it takes at least that long to design and create a new computer chip before it reaches the stores. We run these applications on a simulator, which mimics the behavior of the new processor in order to identify areas where we could improve performance. We then work with logic and circuit designers in order to put changes into the processor to improve its capabilities.

On an average day, I work on the computer simulator using computer programming in the C++ language and analyze such application behavior on the simulator. I also spend time meeting with other team members in my own group and other groups to brainstorm new ideas, devise solutions to current problems, or debug issues that we find.

Q. What advice would you give to high school students who are interested in this career?

A. In order to be an engineer, it is important to take as many math and science classes as possible. In these classes, you learn how to solve problems, which is the most important trait of an engineer. While you may not use every equation that you learn each day in school, you will use the same problem-solving techniques to solve complex tasks on the job. These classes also provide the basics for the engineering courses you will take in college to learn more about career options as an engineer. For computer engineering, classes that introduce you to computer programming would be helpful as well.

Many schools have robotics clubs, physics clubs, or opportunities to participate in "engineering days" off-campus at local universities or companies. These activities give you the opportunity to try engineering through hands-on, fun activities to apply what you are learning in school to solve problems.

Another important trait is teamwork. In the engineering world, large teams work together to complete projects. For the design of a new microprocessor, over 500 people may work together to achieve this goal. In order to work well in a team, you should practice teamwork while in school through a variety of ways. For example, working in groups for lab or science projects, playing on a sports team or in the band, or competing together in a quiz bowl or math competition are all great ways to gain experience working in teams. These groups help you learn how to work in teams, solve conflicts among team members, and leverage each other's strengths when solving problems or working together toward a common goal.

Q. What are the most important professional and personal qualities for computer engineers?

A. Besides teamwork and problem solving that I mentioned above, additional professional qualities that a computer engineer should possess are the abilities to be inventive and to think outside-the-box. For new, cutting-edge products to be designed, engineers need to be creative and innovative to think of new ways to use technology. For example, such creative ideas can lead to new uses for computer chips, such as in people's shoes, or refrigerators, or cars. Creativity helps companies design new products to help people in new ways. It also helps keep the job fun, exciting, and changing on a daily basis.

Being able to manage your time is also very important for a computer engineer. Tasks are complex and require setting goals in order to take small steps toward the final achievement. A computer engineer must manage time between individual contributions (such as design or programming work) with meetings and group sessions where everyone works together or discusses open issues.

Q. **What do you like most and least about your job?**

A. I love working on a product that people will use everyday. Computers are used by billions of people everyday, and I help design the processor that goes inside many of them. I can see the product that I worked on in the local electronics stores, which is pretty exciting. I love solving problems; it is a great feeling to work hard on something and eventually figure it out in order to contribute a new idea or a solution to a problem at work.

One of the most difficult things about being a computer engineer is coming to the realization that you can never know everything and it is okay to ask for help. We are trained as students to be the first to raise our hands and have the right answer, but when working on a difficult problem in industry, it will likely take more than one person to figure out a feasible solution. A microprocessor is a very complex part and is designed in a team so that each person can become an expert in a certain area. However, it is easy to try and convince yourself that you can solve something on your own and waste time, when it would be more efficient to ask for help and work with others.

Also, because the processor is so complex, the design cycle can be long, such as several years to design a brand new computer chip. These long time frames can be frustrating because you are anxious to see your work to completion, but it is worth it when a quality product is complete and is ready for your friends and family to buy!

Industrial Engineers

OVERVIEW

Industrial engineers use their knowledge of various disciplines—including systems engineering, management science, operations research, and fields such as ergonomics—to determine the most efficient and cost-effective methods for industrial production. They are responsible for designing systems that integrate materials, equipment, information, and people in the overall production process. Approximately 192,000 industrial engineers are employed in the United States.

HISTORY

In today's industries, manufacturers increasingly depend on industrial engineers to determine the most efficient production techniques and processes. The roots of industrial engineering, however, can be traced to ancient Greece, where records indicate that manufacturing labor was divided among people having specialized skills.

The most significant milestones in industrial engineering, before the field even had an official name, occurred in the 18th century, when a number of inventions were introduced in the textile industry. The first was the flying shuttle that opened the door to the highly automatic weaving we now take for granted. This shuttle allowed one person, rather than two, to weave fabrics wider than ever before. Other innovative devices, such as the power loom and the spinning jenny that increased weaving speed and improved quality, soon followed. By the late 18th century, the Industrial Revolution was in full swing. Innovations in manufacturing were made, standardization of interchangeable parts was implemented, and specialization of labor was increasingly put into practice.

QUICK FACTS

School Subjects
Computer science
Mathematics

Personal Skills
Leadership/management
Technical/scientific

Work Environment
Primarily indoors
Primarily one location

Minimum Education Level
Bachelor's degree

Salary Range
$43,620 to $66,670 to $97,000+

Certification or Licensing
Required by certain states

Outlook
About as fast as the average

DOT
012

GOE
05.01.06

NOC
2141

O*NET-SOC
17-2112.00

Industrial engineering as a science is said to have originated with the work of Frederick Taylor. In 1881, he began to study the way production workers used their time. At the Midvale Steel Company where he was employed, he introduced the concept of time study, whereby workers were timed with a stopwatch and their production was evaluated. He used the studies to design methods and equipment that allowed tasks to be done more efficiently.

In the early 1900s, the field was known as scientific management. Frank and Lillian Gilbreth were influential with their motion studies of workers performing various tasks. Then, around 1913, automaker Henry Ford implemented a conveyor belt assembly line in his factory, which led to increasingly integrated production lines in more and more companies. Industrial engineers nowadays are called upon to solve ever more complex operating problems and to design systems involving large numbers of workers, complicated equipment, and vast amounts of information. They meet this challenge by utilizing advanced computers and software to design complex mathematical models and other simulations.

THE JOB

Industrial engineers are involved with the development and implementation of the systems and procedures that are utilized by many industries and businesses. In general, they figure out the most effective ways to use the three basic elements of any company: people, facilities, and equipment.

Although industrial engineers work in a variety of businesses, the main focus of the discipline is in manufacturing, also called industrial production. Primarily, industrial engineers are concerned with process technology, which includes the design and layout of machinery and the organization of workers who implement the required tasks.

Industrial engineers have many responsibilities. With regard to facilities and equipment, engineers are involved in selecting machinery and other equipment and then in setting them up in the most efficient production layout. They also develop methods to accomplish production tasks, such as the organization of an assembly line. In addition, they devise systems for quality control, distribution, and inventory.

Industrial engineers are responsible for some organizational issues. For instance, they might study an organization chart and other information about a project and then determine the functions and responsibilities of workers. They devise and implement job evaluation procedures as well as articulate labor-utilization standards for workers. Engineers often meet with managers to discuss cost analysis, financial planning, job evaluation, and salary administration. Not only do they recommend methods for improving employee efficiency but they may also devise wage and incentive programs.

Industrial engineers evaluate ergonomic issues, the relationship between human capabilities and the physical environment in which they work. For example, they might evaluate whether machines are causing physical harm or discomfort to workers or whether the machines could be designed differently to enable workers to be more productive.

REQUIREMENTS

High School

To prepare for a college engineering program, concentrate on mathematics (algebra, trigonometry, geometry, calculus), physical sciences (physics, chemistry), social sciences (economics, sociology), and English. Engineers often have to convey ideas graphically and may need to visualize processes in three-dimension, so courses in graphics, drafting, or design are also helpful. In addition, round out your education with computer science, history, and foreign language classes. If honor level courses are available to you, be sure to take them.

Postsecondary Training

A bachelor's degree from an accredited institution is usually the minimum requirement for all professional positions. The Accreditation Board for Engineering and Technology (ABET) accredits schools offering engineering programs, including industrial engineering. A listing of accredited colleges and universities is available on the ABET's Web site (http://www.abet.org), and a visit here should be one of your first stops when you are deciding on a school to attend. Colleges and universities offer either four- or five-year engineering programs. Because of the intensity of the curricula, many students take heavy course loads and attend summer sessions in order to finish in four years.

During your junior and senior years of college, you should consider your specific career goals, such as in which industry to work. Third- and fourth-year courses focus on such subjects as facility planning and design, work measurement standards, process design, engineering economics, manufacturing and automation, and incentive plans.

Many industrial engineers go on to earn a graduate degree. These programs tend to involve more research and independent study. Graduate degrees are usually required for teaching positions.

Certification or Licensing

Licensure as a professional engineer is recommended since an increasing number of employers require it. Even those employers who do not require licensing will view it favorably when considering new hires or when reviewing workers for promotion. Licensing requirements vary from state to state. In general, however, they involve having graduated from an accredited school, having four years of work experience, and having passed the eight-hour Fundamentals of Engineering exam and the eight-hour Principles and Practice of Engineering exam. Depending on your state, you can take the Fundamentals exam shortly before your graduation from college or after you have received your bachelor's degree. At that point you will be an engineer-in-training. Once you have fulfilled all the licensure requirements, you receive the designation professional engineer.

Other Requirements

Industrial engineers enjoy problem solving and analyzing things as well as being a team member. The ability to communicate is vital since engineers interact with all levels of management and workers. Being organized and detail-minded is important because industrial engineers often handle large projects and must bring them in on time and on budget. Since process design is the cornerstone of the field, an engineer should be creative and inventive.

EXPLORING

Try joining a science or engineering club, such as the Junior Engineering Technical Society (JETS). JETS offers academic competitions in subjects such as computer fundamentals, mathematics, physics, and English. It also conducts design contests in which students learn and apply science and engineering principles. JETS also offers the *Pre-Engineering Times*, a publication that will be useful if you are interested in engineering. It contains information on engineering specialties, competitions, schools, scholarships, and other resources. Visit http://www.jets.org/publications/petimes.cfm to read the publication. You also might read some engineering books for background on the field or magazines such as *Industrial Engineer,* a magazine published by the Institute of Industrial Engineers (IIE). Selected articles from *Industrial Engineer* can be viewed on the IIE's Web site, http://www.iienet.org.

EMPLOYERS

Approximately 192,000 industrial engineers are employed in the United States. Although a majority of industrial engineers are employed in the manufacturing industry, related jobs are found in almost all businesses, including aviation, aerospace, transportation, communications, electric, gas and sanitary services, government, finance, insurance, real estate, wholesale and retail trade, construction, mining, agriculture, forestry, and fishing. Also, many work as independent consultants.

STARTING OUT

The main qualification for an entry-level job is a bachelor's degree in industrial engineering. Accredited college programs generally have job openings listed in their career services offices. Entry-level industrial engineers find jobs in various departments, such as computer operations, warehousing, and quality control. As engineers gain on-the-job experience and familiarity with departments, they may decide on a specialty. Some may want to continue to work as process designers or methods engineers, while others may move on to administrative positions.

Some further examples of specialties include work measurement standards, shipping and receiving, cost control, engineering economics, materials handling, management information systems, mathematical models, and operations. Many who choose industrial engineering as a career find its appeal in the diversity of sectors that are available to explore.

ADVANCEMENT

After having worked at least three years in the same job, an industrial engineer may have the basic credentials needed for advancement to a higher position. In general, positions in operations and administration are considered high-level jobs, although this varies from company to company. Engineers who work in these areas tend to earn larger salaries than those who work in warehousing or cost control, for example. If one is interested in moving to a different company, it is considered easier to do so within the same industry.

Industrial engineering jobs are often considered stepping-stones to management positions, even in other fields. Engineers with many years' experience frequently are promoted to higher level jobs with greater responsibilities. Because of the field's broad exposure, industrial engineering employees are generally considered better prepared for executive roles than are other types of engineers.

EARNINGS

According to the U.S. Department of Labor, the median annual wage for industrial engineers in 2005 was $66,670. The lowest paid 10 percent of all industrial engineers earned less than $43,620 annually. However, as with most occupations, salaries rise as more experience is gained. Very experienced engineers can earn more than $97,000. According to a survey by the National Association of Colleges and Employers, the average starting salary for industrial engineers with a bachelor's degree was $49,567 in 2005, with a master's degree, $56,561 a year; and with a Ph.D., $85,000.

WORK ENVIRONMENT

Industrial engineers usually work in offices at desks and computers, designing and evaluating plans, statistics, and other documents. Overall, industrial engineering is ranked above other engineering disciplines for factors such as employment outlook, salary, and physical environment. However, industrial engineering jobs are considered stressful because they often entail tight deadlines and demanding quotas, and jobs are moderately competitive. Engineers work an average of 46 hours per week.

Industrial engineers generally collaborate with other employees, conferring on designs and procedures, as well as with business managers and consultants. Although they spend most of their time in their offices, they frequently must evaluate conditions at factories and plants, where noise levels are often high.

OUTLOOK

The U.S. Department of Labor anticipates that employment for industrial engineers will grow about as fast as the average for all occupations through 2014. The demand for industrial engineers will continue as manufacturing and other companies strive to make their production processes more effective and competitive. Engineers who transfer or retire will create the highest percentage of openings in this field.

FOR MORE INFORMATION

For a list of ABET-accredited engineering schools, contact
Accreditation Board for Engineering and Technology (ABET)
111 Market Place, Suite 1050
Baltimore, MD 21202-7116
Tel: 410-347-7700
http://www.abet.org

For comprehensive information about careers in industrial engineering, contact
Institute of Industrial Engineers
3577 Parkway Lane, Suite 200
Norcross, GA 30092-2833
Tel: 800-494-0460
http://www.iienet.org

Visit the JETS Web site for membership information and to read the online brochure Industrial Engineering.
Junior Engineering Technical Society (JETS)
1420 King Street, Suite 405
Alexandria, VA 22314-2794
Tel: 703-548-5387
Email: info@jets.org
http://www.jets.org

——— INTERVIEW ———

Bonnie Paris has been an industrial engineer for 10 years. She is currently pursuing a Ph.D. at the University of Wisconsin-Madison. She discussed her career with the editors of Careers in Focus: Engineering.

Q. Why did you decide to become an industrial engineer?
A. I am the first engineer in my family, and before I learned of industrial engineering on a campus visit, I was really torn between studying science and studying literature. The more I learned about industrial engineering the more I was drawn to it. Very simply, industrial engineering is the study of work and how to improve the way things are done. There are many facets of industrial engineering, and you can have a rewarding career at a hospital, manufacturing facility, construction company, airline, post office, insurance company, amusement park, or anywhere else. The focus of my studies and my work is on how to improve

health care delivery processes to make health care safer, more cost effective, and more available. I help others do their job more effectively and help make sure that we provide the best care possible to every patient.

Q. Tell us about the path that you took to become an industrial engineer?

A. As a college student, I looked for jobs that related to my studies such as time studies, work study, and facility layout. While in school, I started working in the process improvement department of a large hospital. When I graduated, I decided to remain at the hospital and take on additional responsibility. During the 10 years I worked at the hospital, my job evolved from conducting studies to mentoring others in how to develop and conduct studies, and I worked on a wide variety of projects. Each project provided me an opportunity to learn something new and meet new people. I worked on projects in materials management, operating room scheduling, patient transportation, food and nutrition, and so on. While working, I went back to school and earned my master's in industrial engineering and then I started teaching night classes in addition to my "day job." I have returned to student life to pursue a Ph.D. in industrial engineering because I want to become a professor and help others learn how to analyze and improve work.

Q. Tell us about your work as a graduate research assistant. On what type of projects do you work?

A. As a research assistant, I work with other researchers to study the impact of using computers to enter medication orders in an intensive care unit setting. I help with collecting data—for example, building a database to hold information collected during the study. I also take classes and do independent research, reading and talking to others about topics that interest me. I wonder how we can use computers to make the "right" information available at the "right" time to people (like doctors and nurses) making decisions. I wonder how we can model and understand a complex job like nursing, where there are physical tasks, mental tasks, time pressures, interruptions, and a lot of emotional aspects. Sometimes I share what I have learned by writing articles or giving presentations.

Materials Engineers

OVERVIEW

Materials engineers extract, process, create, design, and test materials—such as metals, ceramics, plastics, semiconductors, and combinations of these materials called composites—to create a wide variety of products. Approximately 21,000 materials engineers are employed in the United States.

HISTORY

Physical metallurgy as a modern science dates back to 1890, when a group of metallurgists began the study of alloys. Enormous advances were made in the 20th century, including the development of stainless steel, the discovery of a strong but lightweight aluminum, and the increased use of magnesium and its alloys.

Not until the scientific and industrial revolutions of the 19th century did people begin to use ceramics in complex scientific and industrial processes. Individuals skilled with ceramic materials began to develop new, man-made materials to be used in high-technology applications. New uses were also developed for naturally occurring materials, which made possible the development of new products that were stronger, more transparent, or more magnetic. The earliest ceramic engineers used porcelains for high-voltage electrical insulation. Ceramic engineers benefited other industries as well, developing, for example, material for spark plugs (automotive and aerospace industries) and magnetic and semiconductor materials (electronics industry). Today, basic ceramic materials such as clay and sand are being used not only by artists and craftspeople but also by

Metallurgical engineers study computer models on a laptop computer at a job site. *(Index Stock Imagery)*

engineers to create a variety of products—memory storage, optical communications, and electronics.

It was not until 1909 that the Belgian-American chemist Leo H. Baekeland produced the first synthetic plastic. This product replaced natural rubber in electrical insulation and was used for phone handsets and automobile distributor caps and rotors, and is still used today. Other plastics materials were developed steadily. Today, plastics manufacturing is a major industry whose products play a vital role in many other industries and activities around the world. It is difficult to find an area of our lives where plastic does not play some role.

Today, the fields of metallurgical, ceramic, and plastics engineering have become so closely linked that they are now often referred to as materials engineering to reflect their interdisciplinary nature.

THE JOB

Several types of engineering subspecialties exist under the umbrella term, "materials engineer." These include *metallurgical engineers; ceramic engineers;* and *polymer,* or *plastics engineers.*

Metallurgical Engineers

Metals are at the core of every manufacturing society. Parts made from metal are incorporated in a wide variety of products, from steel and iron used in building materials and automobile parts, to aluminum used in packaging, to titanium used in aerospace and military aircraft applications like bulkheads, fasteners, and landing gear. Metallurgy is the art and science of extracting metals from ores found in nature and preparing them for use by alloying, shaping, and heating them.

Metallurgical engineers are specialists who develop extraction and manufacturing processes for the metals industry. Metallurgical engineers develop new types of metal alloys and adapt existing materials to new uses. They manipulate the atomic and molecular structure of materials in controlled manufacturing environments, selecting materials with desirable mechanical, electrical, magnetic, chemical, and heat-transfer properties that meet specific performance requirements. Metallurgical engineers are sometimes also referred to as *metallurgists.*

Ceramic Engineers

Like other materials engineers, ceramic engineers work toward the development of new products. They also use their scientific knowledge to anticipate new applications for existing products.

Ceramic research engineers conduct experiments and perform other research. They study the chemical properties (such as sodium content) and physical properties (such as strength) of materials as they develop the ideal mix of elements for each product's application. Many research engineers are fascinated by the chemical, optical, and thermal interactions of the oxides that make up many ceramic materials.

Ceramic design engineers take the information culled by the researchers and further develop actual products to be manufactured. In addition to working on the new products, these engineers may need to design new equipment or processes in order to produce the products. Examples of such equipment include grinders, milling machines, sieves, presses, and drying machines.

Ceramic test engineers test materials that have been chosen by the researchers to be used as sample products, or they might be involved in ordering raw materials and making sure the quality meets the ceramics industry standards. Other ceramic engineers are involved in more hands-on work, such as grinding raw materials and firing products. Maintaining proper color, surface finish, texture, strength, and uniformity are further tasks that are the responsibility of the ceramic engineer.

Beyond research, design, testing, and manufacturing, there are the *ceramic product sales engineers*. The industry depends on these people to anticipate customers' needs and report back to researchers and test engineers on new applications.

Ceramic engineers often specialize in an area that is associated with selected products. For example, a ceramic engineer working in the area of glass may be involved in the production of sheet or window glass, bottles, fiberglass, tableware, fiber optics, or electronic equipment parts. Another engineer may specialize in whitewares, which involves production of pottery, china, wall tile, plumbing fixtures, electrical insulators, and spark plugs.

Other segments of the industry—advanced, or technical, ceramic—employ a great number of specialized engineers. Areas workers are involved in include engineered ceramics (for things such as engine components, cutting tools, and military armor), bioceramics (for things such as artificial teeth, bones, and joints), and electronic and magnetic ceramics (for products such as computer chips and memory disks).

Plastics Engineers

Today, synthetic polymers—chains of hydrocarbon molecules—represent a multimillion dollar business as either the main ingredient or the item itself in aerospace, building and construction, clothing, packaging, and consumer products. In addition, plastics have had a stunning effect on the automotive, biomedical, communications, electrical and electronic fields, in some cases breathing new life into them.

Plastics engineers perform a wide variety of duties depending on the type of company they work for and the products it produces. Plastics engineers, for example, might design and manufacture lightweight parts for aircraft and automobiles, or create new plastics to replace metallic or wood parts that have come to be too expensive or hard to obtain. Others may be employed to formulate less-expensive, fire-resistant plastics for use in the construction of houses, offices, and factories. Plastics engineers may also develop new types of biodegradable molecules that are friendly to the environment, reducing pollution and increasing recyclability.

Plastics engineers perform a variety of duties. Some of their specific job titles and duties include: *plastics application engineers,* who develop new processes and materials in order to create a better finished product; *plastics process engineers,* who oversee the production of reliable, high quality, standard materials; and *plastics research specialists,* who use the basic building blocks of matter to discover and create new materials.

REQUIREMENTS
High School
While few courses at the high school level are directly related to materials engineering, the basic foundation for engineering includes a wide range of math and science courses. If you are interested in pursuing a career in this field you should invest in an education steeped heavily in math and science, including geometry, algebra, trigonometry, calculus, chemistry, biology, physics, and computer programming. Materials engineers who will also be designing products will need drafting skills, so mechanical drawing and art classes are an excellent choice.

English, speech, and foreign language classes will help you develop strong communication skills and provide you with the opportunity to learn how to better express yourself.

Ancillary interests should not be overlooked. In addition to providing you with possible ways of applying your scientific knowledge in enjoyable, recreational activities, exploring personal hobbies can also develop crucial personal and professional qualities and skills, such as patience, perseverance, and creative problem-solving.

Postsecondary Training

If your career goal is to become a materials engineer, you will need a bachelor of science degree in materials, metallurgical engineering, ceramic engineering, plastics engineering, or a related field. Degrees are granted in many different specializations by more than 80 universities and colleges in the United States.

There are a wide variety of programs available at colleges and universities, and it is helpful to explore as many of these programs as possible, especially those that are accredited by the Accreditation Board for Engineering and Technology (http://www.abet.org). Some programs prepare students for practical design and production work; others concentrate on theoretical science and mathematics. More than 50 percent of materials engineers begin their first job with a bachelor's degree.

Many engineers continue on for a master's degree either immediately after graduation or after a few years of work experience. A master's degree generally takes two years of study. A doctoral degree requires at least four years of study and research beyond the bachelor's degree and is usually completed by engineers interested in research or teaching at the college level.

Certification or Licensing

Licensing is not generally required for most materials engineering professions. However, licensing is recommended to enhance your credentials and make yourself open to more job opportunities.

In general, the licensing process for all branches of engineering results in the formal designation of Professional Engineer (PE). Requirements vary from state to state but generally it takes about four to five years to become a licensed PE. Many engineers begin the process while still in college by taking the Fundamentals of Engineering (FE) exam, an eight-hour test that covers everything from electronics, chemistry, mathematics, and physics to the more advanced engineering issues.

Once a candidate has successfully passed the FE exam, the next requirement to fulfill is to acquire four years of progressive engineering experience. Some states require that materials engineers obtain experience under the supervision of a PE. Once a candidate has four years of on-the-job experience, he or she then takes another exam specific to their engineering area (each branch of engineering has its own specialized, upper-level test). Candidates who successfully complete this examination are officially referred to as Professional Engineers. Without this designation, engineers aren't allowed to refer to themselves as PEs, or function in the same legal capacity as

PEs. For more information on licensing and examination requirements, visit http://www.ncees.org.

Other Requirements

With new products being developed daily, materials engineers are constantly under pressure to integrate new technology and science. Having the imagination to consider all of the possibilities and then being versatile enough to adapt one application of a metal, ceramic, polymer, or other material to another situation are, perhaps, the most essential qualities for materials engineers. To accomplish this, materials engineers must first learn how the material may be applicable to their industry or product line, and then decide how to adjust their current manufacturing process to incorporate it.

In addition to having a good mechanical aptitude for developing parts and tooling, one of the more basic qualities for any student considering a career in materials engineering is a solid understanding of the properties of the material they work with—be it metals, ceramics, polymers, or a composite of these materials.

As in every scientific endeavor, there are always a varying number of factors which influence the outcome of the experiment, and the chemical configurations of a specific material is no different. It takes an individual with an extraordinary amount of patience, focus, and determination to notice precisely what factors are achieving the desired results. Successful materials engineers pay attention to the smallest detail, note the nuances between experiments, and then use that information to develop further tests or theories. Having a certain amount of critical distance helps materials engineers step back from the minutia and reassess the direction in which they're headed.

Materials engineers need to be inquisitive, to take creative steps toward improvements by constantly asking questions, and taking a fresh look at familiar practices.

Good communication skills are vital for success in engineering. You may be required to write reports and present your research before a large audience at industry seminars.

EXPLORING

If you're interested in materials engineering, it's a good idea to take on special research assignments from teachers who can provide guidance on topics and methods. There are also summer academic programs where students with similar interests can spend a week or more in a special environment. It's also a good idea to join a national science club, such as the Junior Engineering Technical Society. In this organization, member students have the opportunity to compete in academic events, take career exploration tests, and enter design contests where they build models of such things as spacecraft and other structures based on their own designs.

For hands-on experience with materials, take pottery, sculpture, or metalworking classes; this will allow you to become familiar with materials such as clay, glass, and metals.

EMPLOYERS

Upon graduation most materials engineers go to work in industry. In industry, materials engineers fall into five main employment groups: manufacturing (where the products are made and tested), material applications and development, machinery/equipment (which requires advanced knowledge of mechanical engineering), government positions, and consulting (where you will need your Professional Engineer licensing).

Approximately 21,000 materials engineers are employed in the United States. Industry employers include aerospace product and parts, computer and electronic products, fabricated metal products, transportation equipment, machinery manufacturing, and primary metal production.

Some materials engineers may continue their studies and go on to teach in higher education. Most materials programs have advanced programs for master's and doctoral studies.

STARTING OUT

As a high school senior, you might want to inquire with established manufacturing companies about internships and summer employment opportunities. College career services offices can also help you find employers that participate in cooperative education programs, where high school students work at materials engineering jobs in exchange for course credits.

Most materials engineers find their first job through their colleges' career services office. Technical recruiters visit universities and colleges annually to interview graduating students and possibly offer them jobs. Materials engineers can also find work by directly applying to companies, through job listings at state and private employment services, or in classified advertisements in newspapers and trade publications.

ADVANCEMENT

In general, advancing through the ranks of materials engineers is similar to other disciplines. Working in entry-level positions usually means executing the research, plans, or theories that someone else has originated. With additional experience and education, materials engineers begin to tackle projects solo or, at least, accept responsibility for organizing and managing them for a supervisor. Those materials engineers with advanced degrees (or, at this point in time, a great deal of experience) can move into supervisory or administrative positions within any one of the major categories, such as research, development, or design. Eventually, those materials engineers who have distinguished themselves by consistently producing successful projects, and who have polished their business and managerial skills, will advance to become the directors of engineering for an entire plant or research division.

EARNINGS

The U.S. Department of Labor reports that materials engineers earned median salaries of $69,660 in 2005. At the low end of the scale, 10 percent of all materials engineers earned less than $44,090 annually in 2005. The highest paid 10 percent had annual incomes of more than $105,330 during this same time period. Starting salaries for those with bachelor's degrees in materials engineering averaged approximately $50,982 in 2005, according to a survey by the National Association of Colleges and Employers. Salaries for government workers are generally less than those who work for private companies.

Materials engineers can expect a good benefits package, including paid sick, holiday, vacation, and personal time; medical coverage; stock options; 401(k) plans; and other perks, depending on the company and industry.

WORK ENVIRONMENT

Working conditions in materials engineering positions vary depending on the specific field and department in which one works. Hands-on engineers work in plants and factories. Researchers work mainly in laboratories, research institutes, and universities. Those in management positions work mostly in offices; and teachers, of course, work in school environments. Whatever the job description, a materials engineer typically works a standard eight-hour day, five days a week. These engineers work indoors, in either an office, a research lab, a classroom, or a manufacturing plant.

OUTLOOK

Employment for materials engineers is expected to grow about as fast as the average through 2014, according to the U.S. Department of Labor. Despite employment declines in many manufacturing industries, materials engineers should continue to have good job prospects. The field of materials engineering is small, and the number of students pursuing study in this discipline is low. This should create opportunities for aspiring materials engineers. Materials engineers will also be needed, of course, to replace those who leave the field for retirement or other work. The U.S. Department of Labor predicts that materials engineers who work with electronics, biotechnology, and plastics products will have good employment prospects. It also predicts that those who specialize in nanomaterials (those at the near-atomic level) and biomaterials (natural or synthetic materials used to manufacture prostheses, implants, and surgical instruments) will have especially strong employment prospects.

FOR MORE INFORMATION

Contact the society for an overview of ceramics, information on student chapters, a list of colleges and universities that offer materials engineering programs, and a list of how ceramics have played a role in the top achievements in engineering.

American Ceramic Society
735 Ceramic Place, Suite 100
Westerville, OH 43081-8728
Tel: 866-721-3322
Email: customerservice@ceramics.org
http://www.ceramics.org

Contact this organization for information on materials engineering careers, scholarships, educational programs, and job listings.

ASM International
9639 Kinsman Road
Materials Park, OH 44073-0002
Tel: 800-336-5152
Email: CustomerService@asminternational.org
http://www.asminternational.org

JETS has career information and offers high school students the opportunity to "try on" engineering through a number of programs and competitions. For more information, contact

Junior Engineering Technical Society Inc. (JETS)
1420 King Street, Suite 405
Alexandria, VA 22314-2794
Tel: 703-548-5387
Email: info@jets.org
http://www.jets.org

The society offers information on ceramics, materials, and metallurgical engineering programs, careers, scholarships, and student chapters.

The Minerals, Metals & Materials Society
184 Thorn Hill Road
Warrendale, PA 15086-7514
Tel: 800-759-4867
Email: tmsgeneral@tms.org
http://www.tms.org

This organization offers information on mining engineering, education, accredited schools, and student membership.

Society for Mining, Metallurgy, and Exploration
8307 Shaffer Parkway
Littleton, CO 80127-4102
Tel: 800-763-3132
Email: cs@smenet.org
http://www.smenet.org

Contact the SPE for information on careers in plastics engineering and scholarships.

Society of Plastics Engineers (SPE)
14 Fairfield Drive
Brookfield, CT 06804-0403
Tel: 203-775-0471
Email: info@4spe.org
http://www.4spe.org

Mechanical Engineers

QUICK FACTS

School Subjects
Computer science
English
Mathematics

Personal Skills
Leadership/management
Technical/scientific

Work Environment
Primarily indoors
One location with some
    travel

Minimum Education Level
Bachelor's degree

Salary Range
$44,550 to $67,590 to
$101,660+

Certification or Licensing
Voluntary (certification)
Required (licensing)

Outlook
About as fast as the average

DOT
007

GOE
05.01.08

NOC
2132

O*NET-SOC
17-2141.00

OVERVIEW

Mechanical engineers plan and design tools, engines, machines, and other mechanical systems that produce, transmit, or use power. They may work in design, instrumentation, testing, robotics, transportation, or bioengineering, among other areas. The broadest of all engineering disciplines, mechanical engineering extends across many interdependent specialties. Mechanical engineers may work in production operations, maintenance, or technical sales, and many are administrators or managers. There are approximately 226,000 mechanical engineers employed in the United States.

HISTORY

The modern field of mechanical engineering took root during the Renaissance. In this period, engineers focused their energies on developing more efficient ways to perform such ordinary tasks as grinding grain and pumping water. Water wheels and windmills were common energy producers at that time. Leonardo da Vinci, who attempted to design such complex machines as a submarine and a helicopter, best personified the burgeoning mechanical inventiveness of the period. One of the Renaissance's most significant inventions was the mechanical clock, powered first by falling weights and later by compressed springs.

Despite these developments, it was not until the Industrial Revolution that mechanical engineering took on its modern form. The steam engine, an efficient power producer, was introduced in 1712 by Thomas Newcomen to pump water from English mines.

More than a half century later, James Watt modified Newcomen's engine to power industrial machines. In 1876, a German, Nicolaus Otto, developed the internal combustion engine, which became one of the century's most important inventions. In 1847, a group of British engineers who specialized in steam engines and machine tools, organized the Institution of Mechanical Engineers. The American Society of Mechanical Engineers was founded in 1880.

Mechanical engineering rapidly expanded in the 20th century. Mass production systems allowed large quantities of standardized goods to be made at a low cost, and mechanical engineers played a pivotal role in the design of these systems. In the second half of the 20th century, computers revolutionized production. Mechanical engineers now design mechanical systems on computers, and they are used to test, monitor, and analyze mechanical systems and factory production. Mechanical engineers realize this trend is here to stay.

THE JOB

The work of mechanical engineering begins with research and development. A company may need to develop a more fuel-efficient automobile engine, for example, or a cooling system for air-conditioning and refrigeration that does not harm the earth's atmosphere. A *research engineer* explores the project's theoretical, mechanical, and material problems. The engineer may perform experiments to gather necessary data and acquire new knowledge. Often, an experimental device or system is developed.

The *design engineer* takes information gained from research and development and uses it to plan a commercially useful product. To prevent rotting in a grain storage system, for example, a design engineer might use research on a new method of circulating air through grain. The engineer would be responsible for specifying every detail of the machine or mechanical system. Since the introduction of sophisticated software programs, mechanical engineers have increasingly used computers in the design process.

After the product has been designed and a prototype developed, the product is analyzed by *testing engineers*. A tractor transmission, for example, would need to be tested for temperature, vibration, dust, and performance under the required loads, as well as for any government safety regulations. If dust were penetrating a bearing, the testing engineer would refer the problem to the design engineer, who would then make an adjustment to the design of the transmission. Design and testing engineers continue to work together until the product meets the necessary criteria.

Once the final design is set, it is the job of the *manufacturing engineer* to come up with the most time- and cost-efficient way of making the product without sacrificing quality. The amount of factory floor space, the type of manufacturing equipment and machinery, and the cost of labor and materials are some of the factors that must be considered. Engineers select the necessary equipment and machines and oversee their arrangement and safe operation. Other engineering specialists, such as chemical, electrical, and industrial engineers, may provide assistance.

Some types of mechanical systems (from factory machinery to nuclear power plants) are so sophisticated that mechanical engineers are needed for operation and ongoing maintenance. With the help of computers, *maintenance and operations engineers* use their specialized knowledge to monitor complex production systems and make necessary adjustments.

Mechanical engineers also work in marketing, sales, and administration. Because of their training in mechanical engineering, *sales engineers* can give customers a detailed explanation of how a machine or system works. They may also be able to alter its design to meet a customer's needs.

In a small company, a mechanical engineer may need to perform many, if not most, of the above responsibilities. Some tasks might be assigned to *consulting engineers,* who are either self-employed or work for a consulting firm.

Other mechanical engineers may work in a number of specialized areas. *Energy specialists* work with power production machines to supply clean and efficient energy to individuals and industries. *Application engineers* specialize in computer-aided design systems. *Process engineers* work in environmental sciences to reduce air pollution levels without sacrificing essential services such as those provided by power stations or utility companies.

REQUIREMENTS

High School

If you are interested in mechanical engineering as a career, you need to take courses in geometry, trigonometry, and calculus. Physics and chemistry courses are also recommended, as is mechanical drawing or computer-aided design, if they are offered at your high school. Communication skills are important for mechanical engineers because they interact with a variety of coworkers and vendors and are often required to prepare and/or present reports. English and speech classes are also helpful. Finally, because computers are such an important part of engineering, computer science courses are good choices.

Postsecondary Training

A bachelor's degree in mechanical engineering is usually the minimum educational requirement for entering this field. A master's degree, or even a Ph.D., may be necessary to obtain some positions, such as those in research, teaching, and administration.

In the United States, there are more than 280 colleges and universities where mechanical engineering programs have been approved by the Accreditation Board for Engineering and Technology. Although admissions requirements vary slightly from school to school, most require a solid background in mathematics and science.

In a four-year undergraduate program, students typically begin by studying mathematics and science subjects, such as calculus, differential equations, physics, and chemistry. Course work in liberal arts and elementary mechanical engineering is also taken. By the third year, students begin to study the technical core subjects of mechanical engineering—mechanics, thermodynamics, fluid mechanics, design manufacturing, and heat transfer—as well as such specialized topics as power generation and transmission, computer-aided design systems, and the properties of materials.

At some schools, a five- or six-year program combines classroom study with practical experience working for an engineering firm or a government agency such as NASA. Although these cooperative, or work-study, programs take longer, they offer significant advantages. Not only does the salary help pay for educational expenses, but the student has the opportunity to apply theoretical knowledge to actual work problems in mechanical engineering. In some cases, the company or government agency may offer full-time employment to its co-op workers after graduation.

A graduate degree is a prerequisite for becoming a university professor or researcher. It may also lead to a higher level job within an engineering department or firm. Some companies encourage their employees to pursue graduate education by offering tuition-reimbursement programs. Because technology is rapidly developing, mechanical engineers need to continue their education, formally or informally, throughout their careers. Conferences, seminars, and professional journals serve to educate engineers about developments in the field.

Certification or Licensing

Engineers whose work may affect the life, health, or safety of the public must be registered according to regulations in all 50 states and the District of Columbia. Applicants for registration must have received a degree from an accredited engineering program and have four years of experience. They must also pass a written examination. For more information on licensing and examination requirements, visit http://www.ncees.org.

Many mechanical engineers also become certified. Certification is a status granted by a technical or professional organization for the purpose of recognizing and documenting an individual's abilities in a specific engineering field. For example, the Society of Manufacturing Engineers offers the following designations to mechanical engineers who work in manufacturing and who meet education and experience requirements: certified manufacturing engineer and certified engineer manager.

Other Requirements

Personal qualities essential for mechanical engineers include the ability to think analytically, to solve problems, and to work with abstract ideas. Attention to detail is also important, as are good oral and written communication skills and the ability to work well in groups. Computer literacy is essential.

EXPLORING

One of the best ways to learn about the field is to talk with a mechanical engineer. It might also be helpful to tour an industrial plant or visit a local museum specializing in science and industry. Public libraries usually have books on mechanical engineering that might be enlightening. You might tackle a design or building project to test your aptitude for the field. Finally, some high schools offer engineering clubs or organizations. Membership in JETS, the Junior Engineering Technical Society (http://www.jets.org), is suggested for prospective mechanical engineers.

EMPLOYERS

Approximately 226,000 mechanical engineers are employed in the United States. Most mechanical engineers work in manufacturing, employed by a wide variety of industries. For example, manufacturers of industrial and office machinery, farm equipment, automobiles, petroleum, pharmaceuticals, fabricated metal products, pulp

Books to Read

Baine, Celeste. *Is There an Engineer Inside You?: A Comprehensive Guide to Career Decisions in Engineering.* Belmont, Calif.: Professional Publications, 2004.

Landels, John G. *Engineering in the Ancient World.* Revised edition. Berkeley, Calif.: University of California Press, 2000.

McGraw-Hill. *Dictionary of Engineering.* 2d ed. New York: McGraw-Hill Professional, 2003.

National Geographic Society. *The Builders: Marvels of Engineering.* Washington, D.C.: National Geographic Books, 1998.

Petroski, Henry. *Engineers of Dreams: Great Bridge Builders and the Spanning of America.* New York: Vintage Books, 1996.

Petroski, Henry. *The Evolution of Useful Things.* New York: Vintage, 1994.

Petroski, Henry. *Invention by Design: How Engineers Get From Thought to Thing.* Cambridge, Mass.: Harvard University Press, 1998.

Pool, Robert. *Beyond Engineering: How Society Shapes Technology.* New York: Oxford University Press, 1999.

Scarl, Donald. *How to Solve Problems For Success in Freshman Physics, Engineering, and Beyond.* 6th ed. Glen Cove, N.Y.: Dosoris Press, 2003.

Scarre, Chris (ed.). *The Seventy Wonders of the Ancient World: The Great Monuments and How They Were Built.* New York: Thames & Hudson, 1999.

Tobin, James. *Great Projects: The Epic Story of the Building of America: From the Taming of the Mississippi to the Invention of the Internet.* New York: The Free Press, 2001.

and paper, electronics, utilities, computers, soap and cosmetics, and heating, ventilating, and air-conditioning systems all employ mechanical engineers. Others are self-employed or work for consulting firms, government agencies, or colleges and universities.

STARTING OUT

Many mechanical engineers find their first job through their college or university career services office. Many companies send recruiters to college campuses to interview and sign up engineering graduates. Other students might find a position in the company where they had a summer or part-time job. Newspapers and professional journals often list job openings for engineers. Job seekers who wish to work for the federal government should contact the nearest branch of the Office of Personnel Management.

ADVANCEMENT

As engineers gain experience, they can advance to jobs with a wider scope of responsibility and higher pay. Some of these higher level jobs include technical service and development officers, team leaders, research directors, and managers. Some mechanical engineers use their technical knowledge in sales and marketing positions, while others form their own engineering business or consulting firm.

Many engineers advance by furthering their education. A master's degree in business administration, in addition to an engineering degree, is sometimes helpful in obtaining an administrative position. A master's or doctoral degree in an engineering specialty may also lead to executive work. In addition, those with graduate degrees often have the option of research or teaching positions.

EARNINGS

The National Association of Colleges and Employers reports the following 2005 starting salaries for mechanical engineers by educational achievement: bachelor's degree, $50,236; master's degree, $59,880; and Ph.D., $68,299. Salaries for mechanical engineers ranged from less than $44,550 to $101,660 or more in 2005, according to the U.S. Department of Labor.

Like most professionals, mechanical engineers who work for a company or for a government agency usually receive a generous benefits package, including vacation days, sick leave, health and life insurance, and a savings and pension program. Self-employed mechanical engineers must provide their own benefits.

WORK ENVIRONMENT

The working conditions of mechanical engineers vary. Most work indoors in offices, research laboratories, or production departments of factories and shops. Depending on the job, however, a significant amount of work time may be spent on a noisy factory floor, at a construction site, or at another field operation. Mechanical engineers have traditionally designed systems on drafting boards, but since the introduction of sophisticated software programs, design is increasingly done on computers.

Engineering is for the most part a cooperative effort. While the specific duties of an engineer may require independent work, each project is typically the job of an engineering team. Such a team might include other engineers, engineering technicians, and engineering technologists.

Mechanical engineers generally have a 40-hour workweek; however, their working hours are often dictated by project deadlines. They may work long hours to meet a deadline, or show up on a second or third shift to check production at a factory or a construction project.

Mechanical engineering can be a very satisfying occupation. Engineers often get the pleasure of seeing their designs or modifications put into actual, tangible form. Conversely, it can be frustrating when a project is stalled, full of errors, or even abandoned completely.

OUTLOOK

The employment of mechanical engineers is expected to grow about as fast as the average for all occupations through 2014, according to the U.S. Department of Labor (USDL). Although overall employment in manufacturing is expected to decline, engineers will be needed to meet the demand for more efficient industrial machinery and machine tools. The USDL predicts good opportunities for mechanical engineers who are involved with new technologies such as biotechnology, nanotechnology, and materials science. It should also be noted that increases in defense spending as a result of the War on Terrorism may create improved employment opportunities for engineers within the federal government.

FOR MORE INFORMATION

For a list of engineering programs at colleges and universities, contact
Accreditation Board for Engineering and Technology
111 Market Place, Suite 1050
Baltimore, MD 21202-7116
Tel: 410-347-7700
http://www.abet.org

For information on mechanical engineering and mechanical engineering technology, contact
American Society of Mechanical Engineers
Three Park Avenue
New York, NY 10016-5990

Tel: 800-843-2763
Email: infocentral@asme.org
http://www.asme.org

For information about careers and high school engineering competitions, contact
Junior Engineering Technical Society
1420 King Street, Suite 405
Alexandria, VA 22314-2794
Tel: 703-548-5387
Email: info@jets.org
http://www.jets.org

For information on certification, contact
Society of Manufacturing Engineers
One SME Drive
Dearborn, MI 48121-2408
Tel: 800-733-4763
Email: service@sme.org
http://www.sme.org

Mining Engineers

OVERVIEW

Mining engineers deal with the exploration, location, and planning for removal of minerals and mineral deposits from the earth. These include metals (iron, copper), nonmetallic minerals (limestone, gypsum), and coal. Mining engineers conduct preliminary surveys of mineral deposits and examine them to ascertain whether they can be extracted efficiently and economically, using either underground or surface mining methods. They plan and design the development of mine shafts and tunnels, devise means of extracting minerals, and select the methods to be used in transporting the minerals to the surface. They supervise all mining operations and are responsible for mine safety. Mining engineers normally specialize in design, research and development, or production. *Mining equipment engineers* may specialize in design, research, testing, or sales of equipment and services. Mines also require *safety engineers*.

There are approximately 5,200 mining and geological engineers employed in the United States.

QUICK FACTS

School Subjects
Earth science
Mathematics

Personal Skills
Mechanical/manipulative
Technical/scientific

Work Environment
Indoors and outdoors
Primarily multiple locations

Minimum Education Level
Bachelor's degree

Salary Range
$43,290 to $70,070 to $119,130+

Certification or Licensing
Required

Outlook
Decline

DOT
010

GOE
05.01.06

NOC
2143

O*NET-SOC
17-2151.00

HISTORY

The development of mining technology stretches back some 50,000 years to the period when people began digging pits and stripping surface cover in search of stone and flint for tools. Between 8000 and 3000 B.C., the search for quality flint led people to sink shafts and drive galleries into limestone deposits.

By about 1300 B.C., the Egyptians and other Near Eastern peoples were mining copper and gold by driving adits (near-horizontal entry tunnels) into hillsides, then sinking inclined shafts from which they drove extensive galleries. They supported the gallery roofs with pillars of uncut ore or wooden props.

Providing adequate ventilation posed a difficult problem in ancient underground mines. Because of the small dimensions of the passageways, air circulated poorly. All methods of ventilating the mines relied on the natural circulation of air by draft and convection. To assist this process, ancient engineers carefully calculated the number, location, and depth of the shafts. At the great Greek mining complex of Laurion, they sank shafts in pairs and drove parallel galleries from them with frequent crosscuts between galleries to assist airflow. Lighting a fire in one shaft caused a downdraft in the other.

Ancient Roman engineers made further advances in the mining techniques of the Greeks and Egyptians. They mined more ambitiously than the Greeks, sometimes exploiting as many as four levels by means of deep connecting shafts. Careful planning enabled them to drive complicated networks of exploratory galleries at various depths. Buckets of rock and ore could be hoisted up the main shaft by means of a windlass. Unlike the Greeks and Egyptians, the Romans often worked mines far below groundwater level. Engineers overcame the danger of flooding to some extent by developing effective, if expensive, drainage methods and machinery. Where terrain allowed, they devised an elaborate system of crosscuts to channel off the water. In addition, they adapted Archimedean screws—originally used for crop irrigation—to drain mine workings. A series of inclined screws, each emptying water into a tub emptied by a screw above it, could raise a considerable amount of water in a short time. It took only one man to rotate each screw, which made it perhaps the most efficient application of labor until engineers discovered the advantage of cutting halls large enough for an animal to rotate the screw. By the first century A.D., the Romans had designed water wheels, which greatly increased the height to which water could be raised in mines.

Mining engineering advanced little from Roman times until the 11th century. From this period on, however, basic mining operations such as drainage, ventilation, and hoisting underwent increasing mechanization. In his book *De Re Metallica* (1556), the German scholar Georgius Agricola presented a detailed description of the devices and practices mining engineers had developed since ancient times. Drainage pumps in particular grew more and more sophisticated. One pump sucked water from mines by the movement of water-wheel-driven pistons.

As mines went deeper, technological problems required new engineering solutions. During the 18th century, engineers devel-

Two mining engineers study rock samples at a coal mine in Wyoming. *(Index Stock Imagery)*

oped cheap, reliable steam-powered pumps to raise water in mines. Steam-powered windlasses also came into use. In the 1800s, engineers invented power drills for making shot holes for rock-breaking explosives. This greatly increased the capability to mine hard rock. In coal mines, revolving-wheel cutters—powered by steam, then by compressed air, then by electricity—relieved miners from the dangerous task of undercutting coal seams by hand. As late as the mid-19th century, ore was still being pushed or hauled through mines by people and animals. After 1900, however, electric locomotives, conveyor belts, and large-capacity rubber-tired vehicles came into wide use so that haulage could keep pace with mechanized ore breaking. The development of large, powerful machines also made possible the removal of vast amounts of material from open-pit mines.

THE JOB

Before the decision is made to mine a newly discovered mineral deposit, mining engineers must go through successive stages of information gathering, evaluation, and planning. As long as they judge the project to be economically viable, they proceed to the next stage. Review and planning for a major mining project may take a decade or longer and may cost many millions of dollars.

First mining engineers try to get a general idea of the deposit's potential. They accomplish this by reviewing geological data, product marketing information, and government requirements for permits, public hearings, and environmental protection. Based on this review, they prepare rough cost estimates and economic analyses. If it appears possible to mine the deposit at a competitive price with an acceptable return on investment, mining engineers undertake a more detailed review.

Meanwhile, geologists continue to explore the mineral deposit in order to ascertain its dimensions and character. Once the deposit has been reasonably well-defined, mining engineers estimate the percentage of the deposit that can be profitably extracted. This estimate, which takes into account the ore's grade (value) and tonnage (volume and density), constitutes the minable ore reserve. It provides mining engineers with enough specific information to refine their economic appraisal and justify further analysis.

At this stage, engineers begin the process of selecting the most suitable mining method—one that will yield the largest profit consistent with safety and efficient ore extraction. In considering the adaptability of mining methods to the deposit, they rely heavily on rock mechanics and geologic data. Measurements of the stresses, strains, and displacements in the rock surrounding the ore body help engineers predict roof-support requirements and settling of rock masses during excavation. Evaluation of the deposit's geologic features (such as the dimensions, inclination, strength, and physical character of the ore and overlying rock) enables engineers to place mine openings in stable rock, avoid underground water, and plan overall excavation procedures. If the evaluation calls for surface mining, engineers must decide where to dig the pits and where to put the rock and soil removed during mining.

Having estimated the ore reserve, chosen a mining method, and begun mine planning, engineers can determine daily (or yearly) mine output tonnage in light of product demand. They also select equipment and help plan and size the mine's plant, support, ore-processing, and shipping facilities.

For underground mining, mining engineers must determine the number and location of mine shafts, tunnels, and main extraction openings. They must also determine the size, number, kind, and layout of the various pieces of equipment. If the project continues to appear economically viable, construction begins.

As actual mine-making proceeds, mining engineers supervise operations. They train crews of workers and supervisors. The stress fields around the mine workings change as the mine expands. Engineers and engineering technicians must inspect the roof of underground cavities to ensure that it continues to have adequate support. Engineers must also continually monitor the quality of air in the mine to ensure proper ventilation. In addition, mining engineers inspect and repair mining equipment. Some mining engineers help plan ways of restoring or reclaiming the land around mine sites so that it can be used for other purposes.

Some mining engineers specialize in designing equipment used to excavate and operate mines. This equipment typically includes ventilation systems, earth- and rock-moving conveyors, and underground railroads and elevators. Engineers also design the equipment that chips and cuts rock and coal. Others select and determine the placement of explosives used to blast ore deposits.

Mining engineers also work for firms that sell mining supplies and equipment. Experienced mining engineers teach in colleges and universities and serve as independent consultants to industry and government.

REQUIREMENTS

High School
To meet the standards set by most engineering colleges, high school students should take as much math and science as possible. Minimum course work includes elementary and intermediate algebra,

plane geometry, trigonometry, chemistry, and physics. Courses in solid geometry, advanced algebra, and basic computer functions are highly recommended. In addition, many engineering colleges require three years of English (preferably emphasizing composition and public speaking) and social science (especially economics and history). Course work in foreign languages also is helpful, because many engineers work overseas.

Postsecondary Training

A bachelor's degree in engineering, preferably with a major in mining engineering, from an accredited engineering program is the minimum requirement for beginning mining engineering jobs. The organization that accredits engineering programs in the United States is the Accreditation Board for Engineering and Technology (ABET). ABET-accredited mining engineering programs assure students that their education will prepare them for professional practice and graduate study.

In a typical undergraduate engineering program, students spend the first two years studying basic sciences, such as mathematics, physics, and chemistry, as well as introductory engineering. Students must also study such subjects as economics, foreign languages, history, management, and writing. These courses equip students with skills they will need in their future work as engineers. The remaining years of college are devoted mostly to engineering courses, usually with a concentration in mining engineering. Engineering programs can last from four to six years. Those that require five to six years to complete may award a master's degree or provide a cooperative engineering education program. Cooperative programs allow students to combine classroom education and practical work experience with a participating mining company or engineering firm.

After completing their formal studies and landing a job, many mining engineers continue their education. They take courses, attend workshops, and read professional journals in order to keep up with developments in their field. Continuing education also enables them to acquire expertise in new technical areas. Some mining engineers pursue advanced degrees. A graduate degree is needed for most teaching and research positions and for many management positions. Some mining engineers pursue graduate study in engineering, business, or law.

Certification or Licensing

Regardless of their educational credentials, mining engineers normally must obtain professional certification in the states in which they work. Professional registration is mandatory for mining engineers whose work may affect life, health, or property or who offer their services to the public. Registration generally requires a degree from an ABET-accredited engineering program, four years of relevant work experience, and passing a state examination. For more information on licensing and examination requirements, visit http://www.ncees.org.

Other Requirements

Certain characteristics help qualify a person for a career in mining engineering. These include the judgment to adapt knowledge to practical purposes, the imagination and analytical skill to solve problems, and the capacity to predict the performance and cost of new processes or devices. Mining engineers must also be able to communicate effectively, work as part of a team, and supervise other workers.

EXPLORING

To learn about the profession of mining engineering, you may find it helpful to talk with science teachers and guidance counselors and with people employed in the minerals industry. You might also wish to read more about the industry and its engineers.

Companies and government agencies that employ graduates of mining engineering programs also hire undergraduates as part of a cooperative engineering education program. Students often enter such programs the summer preceding their junior year, after they have taken a certain

Did You Know?

- The U.S. mining industry employs approximately 300,000 workers.
- There are nearly 14,000 mines in the United States.
- The mining industry has a lower rate of nonfatal injuries and illnesses than the agriculture, construction, or retail industries.
- The average American uses 46,000 pounds of newly mined materials annually.
- More than 35 minerals are used in the manufacture of a computer.
- Telephones are made from as many as 42 different minerals, including aluminum, beryllium, coal, copper, gold, iron, limestone, silica, silver, talc and wollastonite.

Source: National Mining Association

number of engineering courses. They normally alternate terms of on-campus study and terms of work at the employer's facilities.

On the job, students assume the role of a junior mining engineer. They report to an experienced engineer, who acts as their supervisor and counselor. He or she assigns them work within their capabilities, evaluates their performance, and advises them as though they were permanent employees. Students have ample opportunity to interact with a diverse group of engineers and managers and to ask them about their work, their company, and mining engineering in general. Participation in the actual practice of the profession can help students assess their own aptitudes and interests and decide which courses will be most useful to them during the remainder of their engineering program.

EMPLOYERS

There are approximately 5,200 mining and geological engineers employed in the United States. Nearly 50 percent work in the mining industry itself; the others work for government agencies or engineering consulting firms.

STARTING OUT

Beginning mining engineers generally perform routine tasks under the supervision of experienced engineers. Some mining companies provide starting engineers with in-house training. As engineers gain knowledge and experience, they receive increasingly difficult assignments along with greater independence to develop designs, solve problems, and make decisions.

ADVANCEMENT

Mining engineers may become directors of specific mining projects. Some head research projects. Mining engineers may go on to work as technical specialists or to supervise a team of engineers and technicians. Some eventually manage their mining company's engineering department or enter other managerial, management support, or sales positions.

EARNINGS

The U.S. Department of Labor reports that median annual earnings of mining and geological engineers were $70,070 in 2005. Salaries ranged from less than $43,290 to more than $119,130.

According to a 2005 salary survey by the National Association of Colleges and Employers, new graduates with bachelor's degrees in mining and mineral engineering received starting offers averaging $48,643 a year.

Engineers who work for the federal government in its mining operations tend to earn slightly less than their counterparts in private industry.

WORK ENVIRONMENT

Engineers in the mining industry generally work where the mineral deposits are situated, often near small, rural communities. But those who specialize in research, management, consulting, or sales may work in metropolitan areas.

For those who work at the mine sites, conditions vary depending on the mine's location and structure and on what the engineer does. Conditions in the underground environment differ from those in surface mining. Natural light and fresh air are absent; temperatures may be uncomfortably hot or cold. Some mines have large amounts of water seeping into the openings. Potential hazards include caving ground, rockfalls, explosions from accumulation of gas or misuse of explosives, and poisonous gases. Most mines, however, are relatively safe and comfortable, owing to artificial light and ventilation, protective clothing, and water-pumping and ground-support systems.

Many mining engineers work a standard 40-hour week. In order to meet project deadlines, however, they may have to work longer hours under considerable stress.

OUTLOOK

The demand for mining engineers is expected to decline through 2014 because of predicted low growth in the demand for coal, metals, minerals mining, as well as the demand for products made from stone, clay, and glass. Petroleum, natural gas, and nuclear energy are more readily available at more reasonable prices. The employment rate for mining engineers in the United States also depends on the price of coal and metals from other countries.

Despite this prediction, opportunities for mining engineers should be good for several reasons. Many mining engineers are nearing retirement age. Since few students major in mining engineering, these vacant positions may not be completely filled by new graduates. Additionally, U.S. mining engineers are increasingly sought after to work on projects in foreign countries. Mining engineers who are willing to work in foreign countries will have strong employment prospects.

Shortages in our natural resources will also create new opportunities for mining engineers. As mineral deposits are depleted, engineers will have to devise ways of mining less accessible low-grade ores to meet the demand for new alloys and new uses for minerals and metals.

FOR MORE INFORMATION

For statistics on the mining industry, contact
National Mining Association
101 Constitution Avenue, NW, Suite 500 East
Washington, DC 20001-2133
Tel: 202-463-2600
Email: craulston@nma.org
http://www.nma.org

For information on education and student membership, contact
Society for Mining, Metallurgy, and Exploration
PO Box 277002
8307 Shaffer Parkway
Littleton, CO 80127-4102
Tel: 800-763-3132
Email: cs@smenet.org
http://www.smenet.org

For information on careers, schools, college student membership, scholarships and grants, and other resources, contact
The Minerals, Metals, and Materials Society
184 Thorn Hill Road
Warrendale, PA 15086-7514
Tel: 800-759-4867
Email: tmsgeneral@tms.org
http://www.tms.org

Nuclear Engineers

OVERVIEW

Nuclear engineers are concerned with accessing, using, and controlling the energy released when the nucleus of an atom is split. The process of splitting atoms, called fission, produces a nuclear reaction, which creates radiation in addition to nuclear energy. Nuclear energy and radiation has many uses. Some engineers design, develop, and operate nuclear power plants, which are used to generate electricity and power navy ships. Others specialize in developing nuclear weapons, medical uses for radioactive materials, and disposal facilities for radioactive waste. There are approximately 17,000 nuclear engineers employed in the United States.

HISTORY

Nuclear engineering as a formal science is quite young. However, part of its theoretical foundation rests with the ancient Greeks. In the fifth century B.C., Greek philosophers postulated that the building blocks of all matter were indestructible elements, which they named *atomos*, meaning "indivisible." This atomic theory was accepted for centuries, until the British chemist and physicist John Dalton revised it in the early 1800s. In the following century, scientific and mathematical experimentation led to the formation of modern atomic and nuclear theory.

Today, it is known that the atom is far from indivisible and that its dense center, the nucleus, can be split to create tremendous energy. The first occurrence of this splitting process was inadvertently induced in 1938 by two German chemists, Otto Hahn and Fritz Strassman. Further studies confirmed this process and established

QUICK FACTS

School Subjects
Mathematics
Physics

Personal Skills
Communication/ideas
Technical/scientific

Work Environment
Primarily indoors
Primarily one location

Minimum Education Level
Bachelor's degree

Salary Range
$51,182 to $88,290 to $120,540+

Certification or Licensing
Required for certain positions

Outlook
More slowly than the average

DOT
015

GOE
05.01.03

NOC
2132

O*NET-SOC
17-2161.00

that the fragments resulting from the fission in turn strike the nuclei of other atoms, resulting in a chain reaction that produces constant energy.

A nuclear engineer takes equipment readings in a nuclear power control room. *(Index Stock Imagery)*

The discipline of modern nuclear engineering is traced to 1942, when physicist Enrico Fermi and his colleagues produced the first self-sustained nuclear chain reaction in the first nuclear reactor ever built. In 1950, North Carolina State College offered the first accredited nuclear engineering program. By 1965, nuclear engineering programs had become widely available at universities and colleges throughout the country and worldwide. These programs provided engineers with a background in reactor physics and control, heat transfer, radiation effects, and shielding.

Current applications in the discipline of nuclear engineering include the use of reactors to propel naval vessels and the production of radioisotopes for medical purposes. Most of the growth in the nuclear industry, however, has focused on the production of electric energy.

Despite the controversy over the risks involved with atomic power, it continues to be used around the world for a variety of purposes. The Nuclear Energy Institute reports that 30 countries currently operate nuclear energy plants to produce electricity. In the United States, approximately 20 percent of the country's electricity is supplied by nuclear plants. In 2006, Vermont received 72.5 percent of its electricity from nuclear power, the highest of all states. Medicine, manufacturing, and agriculture have also benefited from nuclear research. Such use requires the continued development of nuclear waste management. Low-level wastes, which result from power plants as well as hospitals and research facilities, must be reduced in volume, packed in leak-proof containers, and buried, and waste sites must be continually monitored.

THE JOB

Nuclear engineers are involved in various aspects of the generation, use, and maintenance of nuclear energy and the safe disposal of its waste. Nuclear engineers work on research and development, design, fuel management, safety analysis, operation and testing, sales, and education. Their contributions affect consumer and industrial power supplies, medical technology, the food industry, and other industries.

Nuclear engineering is dominated by the power industry. Some engineers work for companies that manufacture reactors. They research, develop, design, manufacture, and install parts used in these facilities, such as core supports, reflectors, thermal shields, biological shields, instrumentation, and safety and control systems.

Those who are responsible for the maintenance of power plants must monitor operations efficiently and guarantee that facilities meet safety standards. Nuclear energy activities in the United States are closely supervised and regulated by government and independent agencies, especially the Nuclear Regulatory Commission (NRC). The NRC oversees the use of nuclear materials by electric utility companies throughout the United States. NRC employees are responsible for ensuring the safety of nongovernment nuclear materials and facilities and for making sure that related operations do not adversely affect public health or the environment. Nuclear engineers who work for regulatory agencies are responsible for setting the standards that all organizations involved with nuclear energy must follow. They issue licenses, establish rules, implement safety research, perform risk analyses, conduct on-site inspections, and pursue research. The NRC is one of the main regulatory agencies employing nuclear engineers.

Many nuclear engineers work directly with public electric utility companies. Tasks are diverse, and teams of engineers are responsible for supervising construction and operation, analyzing safety, managing fuel, assessing environmental impact, training personnel, managing the plant, storing spent fuel, managing waste, and analyzing economic factors.

Some engineers working for nuclear power plants focus on the quality of the water supply. Their plants extract salt from water, and engineers develop new methods and designs for such desalinization systems.

The food supply also benefits from the work of nuclear engineers. Nuclear energy is used for pasteurization and sterilization, insect and pest control, and fertilizer production. Furthermore, nuclear engineers conduct genetic research on improving various food strains and their resistance to harmful elements.

Nuclear engineers in the medical field design and construct equipment for diagnosing and treating illnesses and disease. They perform research on radioisotopes, which are produced by nuclear reactions. Radioisotopes are used in heart pacemakers, in X-ray equipment, and for sterilizing medical instruments. According to the Nuclear Energy Institute, approximately 4,000 nuclear medicine departments at hospitals across the country perform, on an annual basis, more than 11 million patient procedures.

Numerous other jobs are performed by nuclear engineers. *Nuclear health physicists, nuclear criticality safety engineers,* and *radiation protection technicians* conduct research and training programs designed to protect plant and laboratory employees against radiation hazards. *Nuclear fuels research engineers* and *nuclear fuels reclamation engineers* work with reprocessing systems for atomic fuels. *Accelerator operators* coordinate the operation of equipment used in experiments on subatomic particles, and *scanners* work with photographs, produced by particle detectors, of atomic collisions.

REQUIREMENTS

High School

If you are interested in becoming a professional engineer, you must begin preparing yourself in high school. You should take honors-level courses in mathematics and the sciences. Specifically, you should complete courses in algebra, geometry, trigonometry, and calculus; chemistry, physics, and biology. Take English, social studies, and a foreign language (many published technical papers that are required reading in later years are written in German or French). Be sure to keep your computer skills up to date by taking computer science classes.

Postsecondary Training

Professional engineers must have at least a bachelor's degree. You should attend a four-year college or university that is approved by the Accreditation Board for Engineering and Technology. In a nuclear engineering program, you will focus on subjects similar to those studied in high school but at a more advanced level. Courses also include engineering sciences and atomic and nuclear physics.

These subjects will prepare you for analyzing and designing nuclear systems and understanding how they operate. You will learn and comprehend what is involved in the interaction between radiation and matter; radiation measurements; the production and use of radioisotopes; reactor physics and engineering; and fusion reactions. The subject of safety will be emphasized, particularly with regard to handling radiation sources and implementing nuclear systems.

You must have a master's or doctoral degree for most jobs in research and higher education, and for supervisory and administrative positions. It is recommended that you obtain a graduate degree in nuclear engineering because this level of education will help you obtain the skills required for advanced specialization in the field. Many institutions that offer advanced degrees have nuclear reactors and well-equipped laboratories for teaching and research. You can obtain information about these schools by contacting the U.S. Department of Energy (http://www.energy.gov).

Certification or Licensing

A professional engineer license is usually required before obtaining employment on public projects (i.e., work that may affect life, health, or property). Although registration guidelines differ for each state, most states require a degree from an accredited engineering program, four years of work experience in the field, and a minimum grade on a state exam. For more information on licensing and examination requirements, visit http://www.ncees.org.

Other Requirements

Nuclear engineers will encounter two unique concerns. First, exposure to high levels of radiation may be hazardous; thus, engineers must always follow safety measures. Those working near radioactive materials must adhere to strict precautions outlined by regulatory standards. In addition, female engineers of childbearing age may not be allowed to work in certain areas or perform certain duties because of the potential harm to the human fetus from radiation.

Finally, nuclear engineers must be prepared for a lifetime of continuing education. Because nuclear engineering is founded in the fundamental theories of physics and the notions of atomic and nuclear theory are difficult to conceptualize except mathematically, an aptitude for physics, mathematics, and chemistry is indispensable.

EXPLORING

If you are interested in becoming an engineer, you can join science clubs such as the Junior Engineering Technical Society (JETS), which has a chapter in almost every state. Its publication, *The Pre-Engineering Times* (http://www.jets.org/publications/petimes.cfm), will introduce you to engineering careers and a wide variety of engineering-related resources. If you are a more advanced student, you may want to read materials published by the American Nuclear Society (http://www.ans.org). You may also want to join science clubs, which provide the opportunity to work with others, design engineering projects, and participate in career exploration.

EMPLOYERS

Nuclear engineers work in a variety of settings. According to the U.S. Department of Labor, approximately 36 percent of the approximately 17,000 nuclear engineers employed in the United States work in electric power generation, transmission and distribution; 17 percent for professional, scientific, and technical services firms; and 12 percent for the federal government. Of those who work for the federal government, many are civilian employees of the navy, and most of the rest work for the U.S. Department of Energy. Some nuclear engineers work for defense manufacturers or manufacturers of nuclear power equipment.

STARTING OUT

Most students begin their job search while still in college, collecting advice from job counselors and their schools' career services centers and using organizations and Web sites to find open positions. For example, the Society of Women Engineers (SWE) offers members the opportunity to post their resumes or find job matches through its Web site. Networking with those already employed in the field is an excellent way to find out about job openings. Networking opportunities are available during meetings of professional organizations, such as the SWE's annual national conference.

As with other engineering disciplines, a hierarchy of workers exists, with the chief engineer having overall authority over managers and project engineers. This is true whether you are working in research, design, production, sales, or teaching. After gaining a certain amount of experience, engineers may apply for positions in supervision and management.

ADVANCEMENT

Because the nuclear engineering field is so young, the time is ripe for technological developments, and engineers must therefore keep abreast of new research and technology throughout their careers. Advancement for engineers is contingent upon continuing education, research activity, and on-the-job expertise.

Advancement may also bring recognition in the form of grants, scholarships, fellowships, and awards. For example, the American Nuclear Society has established a Young Members Engineering Achievement Award to recognize outstanding work performed by members. To be eligible for this award, you must be younger than 40 years old and demonstrate effective application of engineering knowledge that results in a concept, design, analysis method, or product used in nuclear power research and development or in a manufacturing application.

EARNINGS

Nuclear engineers with bachelor's degrees earned average starting salaries of $51,182 per year, according to a 2005 salary survey conducted by the National Association of Colleges and Employers. With a master's degree, candidates were offered $58,814.

Nuclear engineers earned a median income of $88,290 in 2005, according to the U.S. Department of Labor. The department also reports that the highest paid 10 percent of nuclear engineers earned more than $120,540, while the lowest paid 10 percent earned less than $63,760 annually. Nuclear engineers working for the federal government had mean earnings of $87,230 in 2005.

Benefits offered depend on the employer but generally include paid vacation and sick days, health insurance, and retirement plans.

WORK ENVIRONMENT

In general, nuclear engineering is a technically demanding and politically volatile field. Those who work daily at power plants perhaps incur the most stress because they are responsible for preventing large-scale accidents involving radiation. Those who work directly with nuclear energy face risks associated with radiation contamination. Engineers handling the disposal of hazardous material also work under stressful conditions because they must take tremendous care to ensure the public's health and safety.

Research, teaching, and design occupations allow engineers to work in laboratories, classrooms, and industrial manufacturing facilities. Many engineers who are not directly involved with the physical maintenance of nuclear facilities spend most of their working hours, an average of 46 hours per week, conducting research. Most work at desks and must have the ability to concentrate on very detailed data for long periods of time, drawing up plans and constructing models of nuclear applications.

OUTLOOK

According to the U.S. Department of Labor, employment for nuclear engineers is expected to grow more slowly than the average for all occupations through 2014. Most openings will arise as nuclear engineers transfer to other occupations or leave the labor force. However, due to the small number of graduates in the field, job opportunities will stay plentiful.

The recent energy crisis in California and the public's growing acceptance of nuclear power is helping to fuel the need for more plants, and will create improved employment opportunities for nuclear engineers in the near future. In addition to working in plants, nuclear engineers will also be needed to work in defense-related areas, to develop medical technology that is nuclear-related, and to study and improve waste management and safety standards.

FOR MORE INFORMATION

For information on scholarships, education, and careers, contact
American Nuclear Society
555 North Kensington Avenue
La Grange Park, IL 60526-5535
Tel: 708-352-6611
http://www.ans.org

For information on student membership, contact
Junior Engineering Technical Society Inc.
1420 King Street, Suite 405
Alexandria, VA 22314-2794
Tel: 703-548-5387
Email: info@jets.org
http://www.jets.org

For a wide variety of career and industry information, contact
Nuclear Energy Institute
1776 I Street, NW, Suite 400
Washington, DC 20006-3708
Tel: 202-739-8000
http://www.nei.org

For career guidance and scholarship information, contact
Society of Women Engineers
230 East Ohio Street, Suite 400
Chicago, IL 60611-3265
Tel: 312-596-5223
Email: hq@swe.org
http://www.swe.org

For information on careers and nuclear power, contact
U.S. Department of Energy
1000 Independence Avenue, SW
Washington, DC 20585-0001
Tel: 800-342-5363
http://www.energy.gov

Optical Engineers

QUICK FACTS

School Subjects
Mathematics
Physics

Personal Skills
Communication/ideas
Technical/scientific

Work Environment
Primarily indoors
Primarily one location

Minimum Education Level
Bachelor's degree

Salary Range
$47,750 to $73,510 to
$110,570+

Certification or Licensing
Required

Outlook
About as fast as the average

DOT
019

GOE
05.01.07

NOC
2133

O*NET-SOC
N/A

OVERVIEW

Optical engineers apply the concepts of optics to research, design, and develop applications in a broad range of areas. Optics, which involves the properties of light and how it interacts with matter, is a branch of physics and engineering. Optical engineers study the way light is produced, transmitted, detected, and measured to determine ways it can be used and to build devices using optical technology.

HISTORY

The study of the properties of light began during the 1600s when Galileo built telescopes to observe the planets and stars. Scientists, such as Sir Isaac Newton, conducted experiments and studies that contributed to the understanding of light and how it operates. Among Newton's many experiments was his work with prisms that separated sunlight into a spectrum of colors. Christiaan Huygens, a Dutch physicist, also conducted important studies to develop a theory that concerned the wave properties of light.

During the 1800s, other physicists and scientists performed research that confirmed Huygens's theory and advanced the study of light even further. By the mid-1800s, scientists were able to measure the speed of light and had developed means to show how color bands of the light spectrum were created by atoms of chemical elements. In 1864, a British physicist, James C. Maxwell, proposed the electromagnetic theory of light.

Two of the most important discoveries of the 20th century were the development of lasers and fiber optics. The first laser was built by an American physicist, Theodore H. Maiman, in 1960. In 1966, it was discovered that light could travel through glass fibers, which led to the development of fiber optic technology.

Optics, the branch of science that studies the manipulation of light, is a growing field. Engineers today work in applications that include image processing, information processing, wireless communications, electronic technology (including compact disc players, high-definition televisions, and laser printers), astronomical observation, atomic research, robotics, military surveillance, water-quality monitoring, undersea monitoring, and medical and scientific procedures and instruments.

THE JOB
Optical engineers may work in any of the many subfields or related branches of optics. Three of the largest areas are physical optics, which is concerned with the wave properties of light; quantum optics, which studies photons, or individual particles of light; and geometrical optics, which involves optical instruments used to detect and measure light. Other subfields of optics include integrated optics, nonlinear optics, electron optics, magneto-optics, and space optics.

Optical engineers combine their knowledge of optics with other engineering concepts, such as mechanical engineering, electrical engineering, and computer engineering, to determine applications and build devices using optics technology. Optical engineers design precision optical systems for cameras, telescopes, or lens systems. They determine the required specifications and make adjustments to calibrate and fine-tune optical devices. They also design and develop circuitry and components for devices that use optical technology. Some optical engineers design and fabricate inspection instruments to test and measure the performance of optics systems. In designing this equipment, they test that all parts perform as required, diagnose any malfunctioning parts, and correct any defects. Together with electrical and mechanical engineers, they work on the overall design of systems using optical components.

In creating a new product using optical technology, optical engineers go through a multistep engineering process. First, they study the application or problem to understand it thoroughly. Then they brainstorm to come up with possible solutions to the problem. After developing a creative concept, engineers transform it into a design or several designs. They work out all of the details and create a computer-generated model or test unit. This model or unit is tested, and any required revisions to the design are made and tested again. This process continues until the design proves satisfactory. The design is then sent to production, and a product is manufactured. The process is completed with marketing of the product.

For some products, an engineer may perform all of these steps except marketing. Other products require a team of engineers and may include other professionals such as industrial designers, technologists, and technicians.

Some optical engineers specialize in lasers and fiber optics. These engineers, also known as *fiber optics engineers* and *laser and fiber optics engineers,* design, develop, modify, and build equipment and components that utilize laser and fiber optic technology. Lasers are used to produce extremely powerful beams of light that can be transmitted through fiber optics, which are hairlike strands of plastic-coated glass fibers. Using this technology, lasers can cut through material as hard as a diamond, travel over long distances without any loss of power, and detect extremely small movements. Lasers also can be used to record, store, and transmit information.

These engineers may be involved in testing laser systems or developing applications for lasers in areas such as telecommunications, medicine, defense, manufacturing, and construction. For example, lasers are used in surgical procedures and medical diagnostic equipment. They are used in manufacturing industries to align, mark, and cut through both metals and plastics. Military applications such as navigational systems and ballistic and weapon systems use laser technology. Other areas where optical engineers use lasers include robotics, holograms, scanning, compact discs, and printing.

Fiber optics engineers may specialize and work within a specific area of fiber optic technology. They may work with fiber optic imaging, which involves using fiber optics to transmit light or images. These engineers also use fiber optics to rotate, enlarge, shrink, and enhance images. A second area of specialization involves working with sensors. These engineers work with devices that measure temperature, pressure, force, and other physical features. A third type of specialization is in communications, where fiber optic networks allow voice, data, sound, and images to be transmitted over cables. This is used in telephone systems, computer networks, and undersea fiber optic communications systems.

Optical engineers use many different types of equipment to perform their work. Among them are spectrometers, spectrum analyzers, digital energy meters, calorimeters, laser power meters, leak detectors, and wattmeters.

REQUIREMENTS

High School

While in high school, take physical science, physics, chemistry, geometry, algebra, trigonometry, calculus, social studies, English, composition, and computer science classes. Courses in computer-aided design are also helpful. Honors classes in science and mathematics are recommended.

Postsecondary Training

A bachelor of science degree in engineering is required to become an optical engineer. Most engineering programs take four or five years to complete. Many students also receive advanced degrees, such as a master of science degree or a doctorate degree, as they are required for higher-level positions.

There are about 120 colleges and universities in the United States and approximately five in Canada that offer classes in optics. Only a very small number of schools, though, offer programs that grant degrees in optical engineering. Most colleges offer degrees in a related field, such as electrical engineering or physics, with a specialization in optics.

Because each college program is unique, classes in optical engineering may be offered through various departments, such as physics, electrical and computer engineering, electronic and electrical engineering, electronics and photonics imaging, optical engineering, or optical science. Some schools emphasize the engineering aspects of optics, whereas others focus on optical science or the research aspects of optics. Optical science varies from optical engineering in that it is more concerned with studying the properties of light and its interaction with matter than in developing applications that utilize optical technology.

Classes vary based on the type of program, but they generally include intensive laboratory experience and courses in mathematics, physics, chemistry, electronics, and geometric and wave optics. Advanced courses may include electro-optics, lasers, optical systems design, infrared systems design, quantum mechanics, polarization, fiber optics communication, and optical tests and measurement.

Some colleges require internships or cooperative work programs during which students work at a related job for one to three semesters. Alternating study with work experience is an excellent way to gain on-the-job experience before graduation and can lead to employment opportunities upon graduation.

A high number of students receive master of science degrees, which generally take two years of additional study beyond a bachelor's degree. Those who plan to work in research generally earn doctorate degrees, which take four years of additional study beyond a bachelor's degree.

Because the types of programs vary, you should thoroughly research and investigate as many colleges as possible. SPIE, the International Society for Optical Engineering, and the Optical Society of America provides a detailed online database of colleges and universities offering optics courses and describes programs and requirements in depth.

Certification or Licensing

All states require engineers to be licensed. There are two levels of licensing for engineers. Professional Engineers (PEs) have graduated from an accredited engineering curriculum, have four years of engineering experience, and have passed a written exam. Engineering graduates need not wait until they have four years experience, however, to start the licensure process. Those who pass the Fundamentals of Engineering examination after graduating are called Engineers-in-Training (EITs), engineer interns, or intern engineers. The EIT certification usually is valid for 10 years. After acquiring suitable work experience, EITs can take the second examination, the Principles and Practice of Engineering exam, to gain full PE licensure. For more information on licensing and examination requirements, visit http://www.ncees.org.

Other Requirements

To become an optical engineer, you need to have a strong foundation in mathematics and physics as well as an inquisitive and analytical mind. You should be good at problem solving, enjoy challenges, and be methodical, precise, and attentive to details. You should be able to work well both individually and with others.

EXPLORING

Students interested in optics can join science and engineering clubs that provide opportunities for experimentation, problem solving, and team building activities. These clubs provide good grounding in science and math principles and the skills students will need as engineers. Ask your science teacher if you can arrange an independent study project. Another way of exploring is through conducting simple experiments on the properties of light. Books on optics often provide instructions for experiments that may be done with a minimum of equipment. Contact your school or local library for books and other resources to explore.

College students may wish to consider joining a student chapter of a professional association such as SPIE or the Optical Society of America. Participation in association events provides an excellent means to meet with professionals working in the area of optical engineering and to learn more about the field. In addition, membership may include a subscription to trade magazines that include interesting and informative articles on optics. Although these associations do charge membership fees, they are relatively inexpensive for college students.

EMPLOYERS

Optical engineers work for companies that produce robotics. They also work in laboratories, hospitals, and universities, as well as in telecommunications and construction. Companies that employ optical engineers can be found in all geographic areas of the country, although some areas have a higher concentration than others. Employers in areas along the Atlantic coast, from Boston to Washington, D.C., and in large metropolitan areas around cities such as San Jose, Los Angeles, Dallas, Houston, and Orlando provide many opportunities for optical engineers.

STARTING OUT

Some students work part time or during the summer during their college years as laser technicians, optics technicians, or in another related technician job. This work experience is not only a valuable learning tool, but it may lead to a full-time employment offer once they complete their education.

Students in an undergraduate or graduate program can learn about job openings through internships or cooperative programs in which they have participated. College career services offices can also be a source of job leads. Professional associations also provide information on companies that are seeking optical engineers. In many cases, new graduates research companies that hire optical engineers and apply directly to them.

ADVANCEMENT

Optical engineers with a bachelor of science degree often start out as assistants to experienced engineers. As they gain experience, they are given more responsibility and independence and move into higher ranked positions. Engineers who show leadership ability, good communication skills, and management ability may advance to project engineers, project managers, team leaders, or other management positions.

Engineers often return to school to obtain advanced degrees, such as a master's or doctorate degree. With advanced training and experience, they can move into more specialized areas of engineering. Some engineers move into areas of research and become principal engineers or research directors. Engineers may also become college professors or high school teachers.

Some engineers move into sales and marketing. Selling optical devices requires a depth of technical knowledge and the ability to explain the features and benefits of a product. Many engineers, after having spent years designing products, are well equipped for this type of work.

Other optical engineers go into business for themselves, either becoming consulting engineers or starting their own design or manufacturing firms.

EARNINGS

Salaries for optical engineers are similar to those of electrical and electronics engineers. According to the U.S. Department of Labor, the median annual earnings of electrical engineers were $73,510 in 2005. The lowest paid 10 percent earned less than $47,750, and the highest paid 10 percent earned $110,570 or more.

Optical engineers can expect to be paid highly for their expertise, partly due to the fact that the demand for their highly technical skills outweighs the supply. According to a survey conducted by *Optics Report,* optical engineers earned an average salary of $95,600 in 2001.

Companies offer a variety of benefits, including medical, dental, and vision insurance; paid holidays, vacation, sick leave, and personal days; life and disability insurance; pension plans; profit sharing; 401(k) plans; and tuition assistance programs. Some companies also pay for fees and expenses to participate in professional associations, including travel to national conventions, annual meetings, and trade shows.

WORK ENVIRONMENT

Optical engineers generally work in comfortable surroundings—usually offices or laboratories. Most facilities are equipped with modern equipment and computer workstations. Most engineers work five-day, 40-hour weeks, although overtime is not unusual, particularly when working on a special project. Some companies offer flexible work policies in which engineers can schedule their own hours within certain time periods. Most engineers work with other engineers, technicians, and production personnel.

OUTLOOK

Employment of optical engineers is expected to grow at a healthy rate through the coming decade. At present, there are more openings for qualified engineers than there are available engineers to fill these positions, so opportunities should be plentiful.

Applications that utilize optics technology are growing steadily and should provide opportunities in many different industries. The use of fiber optics in telecommunications is expanding, providing opportunities for engineers in the cable, broadcasting, computer, and telephone industries. New applications are being developed in many other areas, such as the medical and defense fields. The increasing use of automated equipment in manufacturing is also providing opportunities for optical engineers, particularly in applications involving robotics technology.

FOR MORE INFORMATION

For information on careers and student membership, contact
Lasers and Electro-Optics Society
c/o The Institute of Electrical and Electronics Engineers
445 Hoes Lane
Piscataway, NJ 08854-1331
Tel: 732-562-3891
Email: k.edsell@ieee.org
http://www.i-leos.org

For information on student membership, contact
Optical Society of America
2010 Massachusetts Avenue, NW
Washington, DC 20036-1023
Tel: 202-223-8130
Email: info@osa.org
http://www.osa.org

For information on colleges, scholarships, student membership, and to participate in an online student forum, visit the SPIE Web site.
SPIE—The International Society for Optical Engineering
PO Box 10
Bellingham, WA 98227-0010
Tel: 888-504-8171
Email: spie@spie.org
http://www.spie.org

For information on educational training in optics, visit
Optics Education
http://www.opticseducation.org

For information on optics and careers in the field, visit
Optics For Teens
http://www.opticsforteens.org

For career advice on issues such as networking, interviewing, and job searching in the field of optics, visit the following Web site organized by the Optical Society of America
Work in Optics
http://www.workinoptics.com

Packaging Engineers

OVERVIEW

Packaging engineers design, develop, and specify containers for all types of goods, such as food, clothing, medicine, housewares, toys, electronics, appliances, and computers. In creating these containers, some of the packaging engineer's activities include product and cost analysis, management of packaging personnel, development and operation of packaging filling lines, and negotiations with customers or sales representatives.

Packaging engineers may also select, design, and develop the machinery used for packaging operations. They may either modify existing machinery or design new machinery to be used for packaging operations.

HISTORY

Certain packages, particularly glass containers, have been used for more than 3,000 years; the metal can was developed to provide food for Napoleon's army. However, the growth of the packaging industry developed during the industrial revolution, when shipping and storage containers were needed for the increased numbers of goods produced. As the shipping distance from producer to consumer grew, more care had to be given to packaging so goods would not be damaged in transit. Also, storage and safety factors became important with the longer shelf life required for goods produced.

Modern packaging methods have developed since the 1920s with the introduction of cellophane wrappings. Since World War II, early packaging materials such as cloth and wood have been largely replaced by less expensive and more durable materials such as steel, aluminum, and plastics such as polystyrene. Modern production methods have also allowed for the low-cost, mass production of traditional materials such as glass and paperboard. Government agencies, manufacturers, and designers are constantly trying to improve packaging so that it is more convenient, safe, and informative.

Today, packaging engineers must also consider environmental factors when designing packaging because the disposal of used packages has presented a serious problem for many communities. The United States uses more than 500 billion packages yearly; 50 percent of these are used for food and beverages and another 40 percent for other consumer goods. To help solve this problem, packaging engineers attempt to come up with solutions such as the use of recyclable, biodegradable, or less bulky packaging.

THE JOB

Packaging engineers plan, design, develop, and produce containers for all types of products. When developing a package, they must first determine the purpose of the packaging and the needs of the end users and their clients. Packaging for a product may be needed for a variety of reasons: for shipping, storage, display, or protection. A package for display must be attractive as well as durable and easy to store; labeling and perishability are important considerations, especially for food, medicine, and cosmetics. If the packaging purpose is for storage and shipping, then ease of handling and durability have to be considered. Safety factors are involved if the materials to be packaged are hazardous, such as toxic chemicals or explosives. Finally, the costs of producing and implementing the packaging have to be considered, as well as the packaging material's impact on the environment.

After determining the purpose of the packaging, the engineers study the physical properties and handling requirements of the product in order to develop the best kind of packaging. They study drawings and descriptions of the product or the actual product itself to learn about its size, shape, weight, and color, the materials used, and the way it functions. They decide what kind of packaging material to use and with the help of designers and production workers, they make sketches, draw up plans, and make samples of the package. These samples, along with lists of materials and cost estimates, are submitted to management or directly to the customer. Computer design programs and other related software may be used in the packaging design and manufacturing process.

When finalizing plans for packaging a product, packaging engineers contribute additional expertise in other areas. They are concerned with efficient use of raw materials and production facilities as well as conservation of energy and reduction of costs. For instance, they may use materials that can be recycled, or they may try to cut down on weight and size. They must keep up with the latest developments in packaging methods and materials and often recommend innovative ways to package products. Once all the details for packaging are worked out, packaging engineers may be involved in supervising the filling and packing operations, operating production lines, or drawing up contracts with customers or sales representatives. They should be knowledgeable about production and manufacturing processes, as well as sales and customer service.

After a packaging sample is approved, packaging engineers may supervise the testing of the package. This may involve simulation of all the various conditions a packaged good may be subjected to, such as temperature, handling, and shipping.

This can be a complex operation involving several steps. For instance, perishable items such as food and beverages have to be packaged to avoid spoilage. Electronic components have to be packaged to prevent damage to parts. Whether the items to be packaged are food, chemicals, medicine, electronics, or factory parts, considerable knowledge of the properties of these products is often necessary to make suitable packaging.

Design and marketing factors also need to be considered when creating the actual package that will be seen by the consumer. Packaging engineers work with *graphic designers* and *packaging designers* to design effective packaging that will appeal to consumers. For this task, knowledge of marketing, design, and advertising are essential. Packaging designers consider color, shape, and convenience as well as labeling and other informative features when designing packages for display. Very often, the consumer is able to evaluate a product only from its package.

The many different kinds of packages require different kinds of machinery and skills. For example, the beverage industry produces billions of cans, bottles, and cardboard containers. Often packaging engineers are involved in selecting and designing packaging machinery along with other engineers and production personnel. Packaging can be manufactured either at the same facility where the goods are produced or at facilities that specialize in producing packaging materials.

The packaging engineer must also consider safety, health, and legal factors when designing and producing packaging. Various guidelines apply to the packaging process of certain products and the packaging engineer must be aware of these regulations. Labeling and packaging of products are regulated by various federal agencies such as the Federal Trade Commission and the Food and Drug Administration. For example, the Consumer Product Safety Commission requires that safe packaging materials be used for food and cosmetics.

REQUIREMENTS

High School

During high school, you should take classes that will prepare you for a college engineering education. Concentrate on mathematics, including algebra, geometry, trigonometry, and calculus, as well as sciences, including physics and chemistry. You will also benefit from taking computer science, mechanical drawing, economics, and accounting classes. English, art, computer-aided design, and graphic arts classes are also recommended.

Postsecondary Training

Several colleges and universities offer a major in packaging engineering. These programs may be offered through an engineering school or a school of packaging within a university. Both bachelor of science and master of science degrees are available. It generally takes four or five years to earn a bachelor's degree and two additional years to earn a master's degree. A master's degree is not required to be a packaging engineer, although many professionals pursue advanced degrees, particularly if they plan to specialize in a specific area or do research. Many students take their first job in packaging once they have earned a bachelor's degree, while other students earn a master's degree immediately upon completing their undergraduate studies. A 2005 member survey conducted by the Institute of Packaging Professionals found that 49 percent of respondents had an undergraduate degree and 24 percent had a master's degree.

Students interested in this field often structure their own programs. In college, if no major is offered in packaging engineering, students can choose a related discipline, such as mechanical, industrial, electrical, chemical, materials, or systems engineering. It is useful to take courses in graphic design, computer science, marketing, and management.

Students enrolled in a packaging engineering program usually take the following courses during their first two years: algebra, trigonometry, calculus, chemistry, physics, accounting, economics, finance, and communications. During the remaining years, classes focus on core packaging subjects, such as packaging materials, package development, packaging line machinery, and product protection and distribution. Elective classes include topics concentrating on packaging and the environment, packaging laws and regulation, and technical classes on specific materials. Graduate studies, or those classes necessary to earn a master's degree, include advanced classes in design, analysis, and materials and packaging processes.

Certification or Licensing

The Institute of Packaging Professionals, a professional society, offers two levels of certification: certified professional in training (CPIT) and certified packaging professional (CPP). The CPIT designation is available to college students, recent graduates, and professionals who have less than six years of experience in the field. Requirements for this certification include passing a multiple-choice test and fulfilling one other qualification from the following upon concluding their sixth year in packaging: present a resume of activities, write a professional paper or hold a patent, or pass an essay test. The CPP designation can be earned by those with at least six years of experience in the field (or a combination of education and work experience). In addition to the experience requirement, candidates must pass a multiple choice test and fulfill one other qualification from the following: present a resume of activities, write a professional paper or hold a patent, or pass an essay test. Although certification is not required, many professional engineers obtain it to show that they have mastered specified requirements and have reached a certain level of expertise.

For those interested in working with the specialized field of military packaging technology, the School of Military Packaging Technology offers a program resulting in certification as a military packaging professional. This program is cosponsored by the National Institute of Packaging, Handling, and Logistics Engineers. Generally, a person earns a bachelor of science degree in packaging engineering before taking these specialized courses.

Special licensing is required for engineers whose work affects the safety of the public. Much of the work of packaging engineers, however, does not require a license even though their work affects such factors as food and drug spoilage, protection from hazardous materials, and protection from damage. Licensing laws vary from state to state, but, in general, states have similar requirements. They require that an engineer must be a graduate of an approved engineering school, have four years of engineering experience, and pass the state licensing examination. A state board of engineering examiners administers the licensing and registration of engineers. For more information on licensing and examination requirements, visit http://www.ncees.org.

Other Requirements
Packaging engineers should have the ability to solve problems and think analytically and creatively. They must work well with people, both as a leader and as a team player. They should also be able to write and speak well in order to deal effectively with other workers and customers, and in order to document procedures and policies. In addition, a packaging engineer should have the ability to manage projects and people.

EXPLORING

To get firsthand experience in the packaging industry, you can call local manufacturers to see how they handle and package their products. Often, factories will allow visitors to tour their manufacturing and packaging facilities.

Another way to learn about packaging is by observing the packaging that you encounter every day, such as containers for food, beverages, cosmetics, and household goods. Visit stores to see how products are packaged, stored, or displayed. Notice the shape and labeling on the container, its ease of use, durability for storage, convenience of opening and closing, disposability, and attractiveness.

You may also explore your aptitude and interest in a packaging career through graphic design courses, art classes that include construction activities, and computer-aided design classes. Participating in hobbies that include designing and constructing objects from different types of materials can also be beneficial. You can also learn about the industry by reading trade publications or visiting their Web sites, such as *Packaging World* (http://www.packworld.com) and *Packaging Digest* (http://www.packagingdigest.com).

EMPLOYERS

Packaging engineers are employed by almost every manufacturing industry. Pharmaceutical, beverage, cosmetics, and food industries are major employers of packaging engineers. Some packaging engineers are hired to design and develop packaging while others oversee the actual production of the packages. Some companies have their own packaging facilities while other companies subcontract the packaging to specialized packing firms. Manufacturing and packaging companies can be large, multinational enterprises that manufacture, package, and distribute numerous products, or they can be small operations that are limited to the production of one or two specific products. Specialized packaging companies hire employees for all aspects of the packaging design and production process. Worldwide manufacturing offers career opportunities around the world. The federal government and the armed services also have employment opportunities for packaging engineers.

STARTING OUT

College graduates with a degree in packaging or a related field of engineering should find it easy to get jobs as the packaging industry continues its rapid growth. Many companies send recruiters to college campuses to meet with graduating students and interview them for positions with their companies. Students can also learn about employment possibilities through their schools' placement services, job fairs, classified advertisements in newspapers and trade publications, and referrals from teachers. Students who have participated in an internship or work-study program through a college may learn about employment opportunities through contacts with industry professionals.

Students can also research companies they are interested in working for and apply directly to the person in charge of packaging or the personnel office.

ADVANCEMENT

Beginning packaging engineers generally do routine work under the supervision of experienced engineers and may also receive some formal training through their company. As they become more experienced, they are given more difficult tasks and more independence in solving problems, developing designs, or making decisions.

Some companies provide structured programs in which packaging engineers advance through a sequence of positions to more advanced packaging engineering positions. For example, an entry-level engineer might start out by producing engineering layouts to assist product designers, advance to the position of product designer, and ultimately move into a management position.

Packaging engineers may advance from being a member of a team to a project supervisor or department manager. Qualified packaging engineers may advance through their department to become a manager or vice president of their company. To advance to a management position, the packaging engineer must demonstrate good technical and production skills and managerial ability. After years of experience, a packaging engineer might wish to become self-employed as a packaging consultant.

To improve chances for advancement, the packaging engineer may wish to get a master's degree in another branch of engineering or in business administration. Many executives in government and industry began their careers as engineers. Some engineers become patent attorneys by combining a law degree with their technical and scientific knowledge.

Many companies encourage continuing education throughout one's career and provide training opportunities in the form of in-house seminars and outside workshops. Taking advantage of any training offered helps one to develop new skills and learn technical information that can increase chances for advancement. Many companies also encourage their employees to participate in professional association activities. Membership and involvement in professional associations are valuable ways to stay current on new trends within the industry, to familiarize oneself with what other companies are doing, and to make contacts with other professionals in the industry. Many times, professionals learn about opportunities for advancement in new areas or at different companies through the contacts they have made at association events.

EARNINGS

Salaries for packaging engineers vary based on factors such as the industry in which they work (food and beverage, pharmaceuticals, cosmetics, personal care, etc.), the size of the employer, the area of the country in which they live, and their years of professional experience. Currently, the average starting salary for a packaging engineer with a bachelor's degree is about $35,000 per year. The mid-range salary is $45,000, with packaging engineers easily earning $90,000 or more as they gain experience and advance within a company.

A member survey conducted by the Institute of Packaging Professionals found that the average respondent earned an annual salary of $75,000 in 2005. Benefits vary from company to company but can include any of the following: medical, dental, and life insurance; paid vacations, holidays, and sick days; profit sharing; 401(k) plans; bonus and retirement plans; and educational assistance programs. Some employers pay fees and expenses for participation in professional associations.

Postsecondary Packaging Education Programs in the United States

Christian Brothers University (Memphis, Tenn.)
901-321-3418
http://www.cbu.edu/engineering/packaging
Degrees available: Certificate

Clemson University (Clemson, S.C.)
864-656-7637
http://www.clemson.edu/packaging
Degrees available: Bachelor's degree, master's degree

University of Florida (Gainesville)
352-392-1864, ext. 111
http://www.agen.ufl.edu/academics/undergrad/PKG.php
Degrees available: Bachelor's degree

University of Illinois-Urbana-Champaign
217-333-3570
http://www.age.uiuc.edu
Degrees available: Bachelor's degree

Indiana State University (Terre Haute)
812-237-3353
http://www.indstate.edu/imt/IMT/bs_pt.htm
Degrees available: Bachelor's degree

Michigan State University (East Lansing)
517-355-9580
http://packaging.msu.edu
Degrees available: Bachelor's degree, master's degree, doctorate
  degree

Rochester Institute of Technology (Rochester, N.Y.)
585-475-7070
http://www.rit.edu/~703www
Degrees available: Bachelor's degree, master's degree

University of Wisconsin-Stout (Menomonie)
715-232-1107
http://www.uwstout.edu/programs/bsp
Degrees available: Bachelor's degree

WORK ENVIRONMENT

The working conditions for packaging engineers vary with the employer and with the tasks of the engineer. Those who work for companies that make packaging materials or who direct packaging operations might work around noisy machinery. Generally, they have offices near the packaging operations where they consult with others in their department, such as packaging machinery technicians and other engineers.

Packaging engineers also work with nontechnical staff such as designers, artists, and marketing and financial people. Packaging engineers must be alert to keeping up with new trends in marketing and technological developments.

Most packaging engineers have a five-day, 40-hour workweek, although overtime is not unusual. In some companies, particularly during research and design stages, product development, and the start up of new methods or equipment, packaging engineers may work 10-hour days or longer and work on weekends.

Some travel may be involved, especially if the packaging engineer is also involved in sales. Also, travel between plants may be necessary to coordinate packaging operations. At various stages of developing packaging, the packaging engineer will probably be engaged in hands-on activities. These activities involve handling objects, working with machinery, carrying light loads, and using a variety of tools, machines, and instruments.

The work of packaging engineers also involves other, social concerns such as consumer protection, environmental pollution, and conservation of natural resources. Packaging engineers are constantly searching for safer, tamper-proof packaging, especially because harmful substances have been found in some food, cosmetics, and drugs. They also experiment with new packaging materials and utilize techniques to conserve resources and reduce the disposal problem. Many environmentalists are concerned with managing the waste from discarded packages. Efforts are being made to stop littering; to recycle bottles, cans, and other containers; and to use more biodegradable substances in packaging materials. The qualified packaging engineer, then, will have a broad awareness of social issues.

OUTLOOK

The packaging industry, which employs more than a million people, offers almost unlimited opportunities for packaging engineers. Packaging engineers work in almost any industry because virtually all manufactured products need one or more kinds of packaging. Some of the industries with the fastest growing packaging needs are food, drugs, and cosmetics.

The demand for packaging engineers is expected to be strong as newer, faster ways of packaging are continually being sought to meet the needs of economic growth, world trade expansion, and the environment. Increased efforts are also being made to develop packaging that is easy to open for the growing aging population and those persons with disabilities.

FOR MORE INFORMATION

For information on certification, contact
Institute of Packaging Professionals
1601 North Bond Street, Suite 101
Naperville, IL 60563-0114
Tel: 630-544-5050
Email: info@iopp.net
http://www.iopp.org

For information on schools with packaging curriculum, contact
National Institute of Packaging, Handling, and Logistics
   Engineers
177 Fairsom Court
Lewisburg, PA 17837-6844
Tel: 570-523-6475
Email: niphle@dejazzd.com
http://www.niphle.org

For industry information, contact
Packaging Machinery Manufacturers Institute
4350 North Fairfax Drive, Suite 600
Arlington, VA 22203-1632
Tel: 888-275-7664
Email: pmmiwebhelp@PMMI.org
http://www.pmmi.org

For information on certification as a military packaging professional, contact
School of Military Packaging Technology
http://smpt.apg.army.mil

Petroleum Engineers

QUICK FACTS

School Subjects
Mathematics
Physics

Personal Skills
Helping/teaching
Technical/scientific

Work Environment
Indoors and outdoors
One location with some
travel

Minimum Education Level
Bachelor's degree

Salary Range
$51,410 to $93,000 to
$145,600+

Certification or Licensing
Required for certain positions

Outlook
Decline

DOT
010

GOE
05.01.08

NOC
2145

O*NET-SOC
17-2171.00

OVERVIEW

Petroleum engineers apply the principles of geology, physics, and the engineering sciences to the recovery, development, and processing of petroleum. As soon as an exploration team has located an area that could contain oil or gas, petroleum engineers begin their work, which includes determining the best location for drilling new wells, as well as the economic feasibility of developing them. They are also involved in operating oil and gas facilities, monitoring and forecasting reservoir performance, and utilizing enhanced oil recovery techniques that extend the life of wells. There are approximately 16,000 petroleum engineers employed in the United States.

HISTORY

Within a broad perspective, the history of petroleum engineering can be traced back hundreds of millions of years to when the remains of plants and animals blended with sand and mud and transformed into rock. It is from this ancient underground rock that petroleum is taken, for the organic matter of the plants and animals decomposed into oil during these millions of years and accumulated into pools deep underground.

In primitive times, people did not know how to drill for oil; instead, they collected the liquid substance after it had seeped to aboveground surfaces. Petroleum is known to have been used at that time for caulking ships and for concocting medicines.

Petroleum engineering as we know it today was not established until the mid-1800s, an incredibly long time after the fundamental ingredients of petroleum were deposited within the earth. In 1859, the American Edwin Drake was the first person to ever pump the so-called rock oil from under the ground, an endeavor that, before its success, was laughed at and considered impossible. Forward-thinking investors, however, had believed in the operation and thought that underground oil could be used as inexpensive fluid for lighting lamps and for lubricating machines (and therefore could make them rich). The drilling of the first well, in Titusville, Pennsylvania (1869), ushered in a new worldwide era: the oil age.

At the turn of the century, petroleum was being distilled into kerosene, lubricants, and wax. Gasoline was considered a useless by-product and was run off into rivers as waste. However, this changed with the invention of the internal combustion engine and the automobile. By 1915 there were more than half a million cars in the United States, virtually all of them powered by gasoline.

Edwin Drake's drilling operation struck oil 70 feet below the ground. Since that time, technological advances have been made, and the professional field of petroleum engineering has been established. Today's operations drill as far down as six miles. Because the United States began to rely so much on oil, the country contributed significantly to creating schools and educational programs in this engineering discipline. The world's first petroleum engineering curriculum was devised in the United States in 1914. Today there are approximately 30 U.S. universities that offer petroleum engineering degrees.

The first schools were concerned mainly with developing effective methods of locating oil sites and with devising efficient machinery for drilling wells. Over the years, as sites have been depleted, engineers have been more concerned with formulating methods for extracting as much oil as possible from each well. Today's petroleum engineers focus on issues such as computerized drilling operations; however, because usually only about 40 to 60 percent of each site's oil is extracted, engineers must still deal with designing optimal conditions for maximum oil recovery.

THE JOB

Petroleum engineer is a rather generalized title that encompasses several specialties, each one playing an important role in ensuring the safe and productive recovery of oil and natural gas. In general, petroleum engineers are involved in the entire process of oil recovery, from preliminary steps, such as analyzing cost factors, to the last stages, such as monitoring the production rate and then repacking the well after it has been depleted.

Petroleum engineering is closely related to the separate engineering discipline of geoscience engineering. Before petroleum engineers can begin work on an oil reservoir, prospective sites must be sought by *geological engineers*, along with *geologists* and *geophysicists*. These scientists determine whether a site has potential oil. Petroleum engineers develop plans for drilling. Drilling is usually unsuccessful, with eight out of 10 test wells being "dusters" (dry wells) and only one of the remaining two test wells having enough oil to be commercially producible. When a significant amount of oil is discovered, engineers can begin their work of maximizing oil production at the site. The development company's *engineering manager* oversees the activities of the various petroleum engineering specialties, including reservoir engineers, drilling engineers, and production engineers.

Reservoir engineers use the data gathered by the previous geoscience studies and estimate the actual amount of oil that will be extracted from the reservoir. It is the reservoir engineers who determine whether the oil will be taken by primary methods (simply pumping the oil from the field) or by enhanced methods (using additional energy such as water pressure to force the oil up). The reservoir engineer is responsible for calculating the cost of the recovery process relative to the expected value of the oil produced and simulates future performance using sophisticated computer models. Besides performing studies of existing company-owned oil fields, reservoir engineers also evaluate fields the company is thinking of buying.

Drilling engineers work with geologists and drilling contractors to design and supervise drilling operations. They are the engineers involved with the actual drilling of the well. They ask: What will be the best methods for penetrating the earth? It is the responsibility of these workers to supervise the building of the derrick (a platform, constructed over the well, that holds the hoisting devices), choose the equipment, and plan the drilling methods. Drilling engineers must have a thorough understanding of the geological sciences so that they can know, for instance, how much stress to place on the rock being drilled.

Production engineers determine the most efficient methods and equipment to optimize oil and gas production. For example, they establish the proper pumping unit configuration and perform tests to determine well fluid levels and pumping load. They plan field workovers and well stimulation techniques such as secondary and tertiary recovery (for example, injecting steam, water, or a special recovery fluid) to maximize field production.

Various research personnel are involved in this field; some are more specialized than others. They include the *research chief engineer,* who directs studies related to the design of new drilling and production methods, the *oil-well equipment research engineer,* who directs research to design improvements in oil-well machinery and devices, and the *oil-field equipment test engineer,* who conducts experiments to determine the effectiveness and safety of these improvements.

In addition to all of the above, sales personnel play an important part in the petroleum industry. *Oil-well equipment and services sales engineers* sell various types of equipment and devices used in all stages of oil recovery. They provide technical support and service to their clients, including oil companies and drilling contractors.

REQUIREMENTS

High School

In high school, you can prepare for college engineering programs by taking courses in mathematics, physics, chemistry, geology, and computer science. Economics, history, and English are also highly recommended because these subjects will improve your communication and management skills. Mechanical drawing and foreign languages are also helpful.

Postsecondary Training

A bachelor's degree in engineering is the minimum requirement. In college, you can follow either a specific petroleum engineering curriculum or a program in a closely related field, such as geophysics or mining engineering. In the United States, there are approximately 30 universities and colleges that offer programs that concentrate on petroleum engineering, many of which are located in California and Texas. The first two years toward the bachelor of science degree involve the study of many of the same subjects taken in high school, only at an advanced level, as well as basic engineering courses. In the junior and senior years, students take more specialized courses: geology, formation evaluation, properties of reservoir rocks and fluids, well drilling, properties of reservoir fluids, petroleum production, and reservoir analysis.

Because the technology changes so rapidly, many petroleum engineers continue their education to receive a master's degree and then a doctorate. Petroleum engineers who have earned advanced degrees command higher salaries and often are eligible for better advancement opportunities. Those who work in research and teaching positions are usually required to have these higher credentials.

Students considering an engineering career in the petroleum industry should be aware that the industry uses all kinds of engineers. People with chemical, electrical, geoscience, mechanical, environmental, and other engineering degrees are also employed in this field.

Certification or Licensing

Many jobs, especially public projects, require that the engineer be licensed as a professional engineer. To be licensed, candidates must have a degree from an engineering program accredited by the Accreditation Board for Engineering and Technology. Additional requirements for obtaining the license vary from state to state, but all applicants must take an exam and have several years of related experience on the job or in teaching. For more information on licensing and examination requirements, visit http://www.ncees.org.

Other Requirements

Students thinking about this career should enjoy science and math. You need to be a creative problem-solver who likes to come up with new ways to get things done and try them out. You need to be curious, wanting to know why and how things are done. You also need to be a logical thinker with a capacity for detail, and you must be a good communicator who can work well with others.

EXPLORING

One of the most satisfying ways to explore this occupation is to participate in Junior Engineering Technical Society (JETS) programs. JETS participants enter engineering design and problem-solving contests and learn team development skills, often with an engineering mentor. Science fairs and clubs also offer fun and challenging ways to learn about engineering.

Certain students are able to attend summer programs held at colleges and universities that focus on material not traditionally offered in high school. Usually these programs include recreational activities such as basketball, swimming, and track and field. For example, Worcester Polytechnic Institute offers the Frontiers program, a two-week residential session for high school seniors. For more information, visit http://www.admissions.wpi.edu/Frontiers. The American Indian Science and Engineering Society (AISES) also sponsors two-to six-week mathematics and science camps that are open to Native American students and held at various college campuses. For more information, visit http://www.aises.org.

Talking with someone who has worked as a petroleum engineer would also be a very helpful and inexpensive way of exploring this field. One good way to find an experienced person to talk to is through Internet sites that feature career areas to explore, industry message boards, and mailing lists.

You can also explore this career by touring oilfields or corporate sites (contact the public relations department of oil companies for more information), or you can try to land a temporary or summer job in the petroleum industry on a drilling and production crew. Trade journals, high school guidance counselors, the career services office at technical or community colleges, and the associations listed at the end of this article are other helpful resources that will help you learn more about the career of petroleum engineer.

EMPLOYERS

Petroleum engineers are employed by major oil companies, as well as smaller oil companies. They work in oil exploration and production. Some petroleum engineers are employed by consulting companies and equipment suppliers. The federal government is also an employer of engineers. In the United States, oil or natural gas is produced in 32 states, with most sites located in Texas, Louisiana, California, and Oklahoma, plus offshore regions. Many other engineers work in other oil-producing areas such as the Arctic Circle, China's Tarim Basin, and the Middle East. Approximately 15,000 petroleum engineers are employed in the United States.

STARTING OUT

The most common and perhaps the most successful way to obtain a petroleum engineering job is to apply for positions through the career services office at the college you attend. Oil companies often have recruiters who seek potential graduates while they are in their last year of engineering school.

Applicants are also advised to simply check the job sections of major newspapers and apply directly to companies seeking employees. They should also keep informed of the general national employment outlook in this industry by reading trade and association journals, such as the Society of Petroleum Engineers' *Journal of Petroleum Technology.*

Engineering internships and co-op programs where students attend classes for a portion of the year and then work in an engineering-related job for the remainder of the year allow students to graduate with valuable work experience sought by employers. Many times these students are employed full time after graduation at the place where they had their internship or co-op job.

As in most engineering professions, entry-level petroleum engineers first work under the supervision of experienced professionals for a number of years. New engineers usually are assigned to a field location where they learn different aspects of field petroleum engineering. Initial responsibilities may include well productivity, reservoir and enhanced recovery studies, production equipment and application design, efficiency analyses, and economic evaluations. Field assignments are followed by other opportunities in regional and headquarters offices.

ADVANCEMENT

After several years working under professional supervision, engineers can begin to move up to higher levels. Workers often formulate a choice of direction during their first years on the job. In the operations division, petroleum engineers can work their way up from the field to district, division, and then operations manager. Some engineers work through various engineering positions from field engineer to staff, then division, and finally chief engineer on a project. Some engineers may advance into top executive management. In any position, however, continued enrollment in educational courses is usually required to keep abreast of technological progress and changes. After about four years of work experience, engineers usually apply for a PE license so they can be certified to work on a larger number of projects.

Others get their master's or doctoral degree so they can advance to more prestigious research engineering, university-level teaching, or consulting positions. Also, petroleum engineers may transfer to many other occupations, such as economics, environmental management, and groundwater hydrology. Finally, some entrepreneurial-minded workers become independent operators and owners of their own oil companies.

EARNINGS

Petroleum engineers with a bachelor's degree earned average starting salaries of $61,516 in 2005, according to the National Association of Colleges and Employers. A survey by the Society of Petroleum Engineers reports that its worldwide members earned an average salary

Earnings By Industry

Field	Mean Annual Earnings
Oil and gas extraction	$107,990
Architectural and engineering services	$102,640
Management and technical consulting services	$91,000
Petroleum and coal products manufacturing	$90,900
Support activities for mining	$80,150

Source: U.S. Department of Labor, 2005

of $116,834 in 2006. Petroleum engineers in the United States with a master's or doctorate degree earned an average salary of $122,570 in 2006. The survey also reports the following average salaries in 2006 for U.S. petroleum engineers by years of experience: zero to 10 years, $85,482; 16 to 20 years, $126,501; and 26 or more years, $137,000.

Salary rates tend to reflect the economic health of the petroleum industry as a whole. When the price of oil is high, salaries can be expected to grow; low oil prices often result in stagnant wages.

Fringe benefits for petroleum engineers are good. Most employers provide health and accident insurance, sick pay, retirement plans, profit-sharing plans, and paid vacations. Education benefits are also competitive.

WORK ENVIRONMENT

Petroleum engineers work all over the world: the high seas, remote jungles, vast deserts, plains, and mountain ranges. Petroleum engineers who are assigned to remote foreign locations may be separated from their families for long periods of time or be required to resettle their families when new job assignments arise. Those working overseas may live in company-supplied housing.

Some petroleum engineers, such as drilling engineers, work primarily out in the field at or near drilling sites in all kinds of weather and environments. The work can be dirty and dangerous. Responsibilities such as making reports, conducting studies of data, and analyzing costs are usually tended to in offices either away from the site or in temporary work trailers.

Other engineers work in offices in cities of varying sizes, with only occasional visits to an oil field. Research engineers work in laboratories much of the time, while those who work as professors spend most of their time on campuses. Workers involved in economics, management, consulting, and government service tend to spend their work time exclusively indoors.

OUTLOOK

Employment for petroleum engineers is expected to decline through 2014, according to the U.S. Department of Labor. Despite this prediction, opportunities for petroleum engineers will exist because the number of degrees granted in petroleum engineering is low, leaving more job openings than there are qualified candidates. (According to the Society of Petroleum Engineers, the average age of its members is 52.) Additionally, employment opportunities may improve as a result of the federal government's plans to construct new gas refineries, pipelines, and transmission lines, as well as to drill in areas that were previously off-limits to such development.

The challenge for petroleum engineers in the past decade has been to develop technology that lets drilling and production be economically feasible even in the face of low oil prices. For example, engineers had to rethink how they worked in deep water. They used to believe deep wells would collapse if too much oil was pumped out at once. But the high costs of working in deep water plus low oil prices made low volumes uneconomical. So engineers learned how to boost oil flow by slowly increasing the quantities wells pumped by improving valves, pipes, and other equipment used. Engineers have also cut the cost of deep-water oil and gas production in the Gulf of Mexico, predicted to be one of the most significant exploration hot spots in the world for the next decade, by placing wellheads on the ocean floor instead of on above-sea production platforms.

Cost-effective technology that permits new drilling and increases production will continue to be essential in the profitability of the oil industry. Therefore, petroleum engineers will continue to have a vital role to play, even in this age of streamlined operations and company restructurings.

FOR MORE INFORMATION

For information on careers in petroleum geology, contact
American Association of Petroleum Geologists
PO Box 979
Tulsa, OK 74101-0979
Tel: 800-364-2274
http://www.aapg.org

For information on summer programs, contact
American Indian Science and Engineering Society
PO Box 9828
Albuquerque, NM 87119-9828
Tel: 505-765-1052
Email: info@aises.org
http://www.aises.org

For general information on the petroleum industry, contact
American Petroleum Institute
1220 L Street, NW
Washington, DC 20005-4070
Tel: 202-682-8000
http://www.api.org

For information about JETS programs, products, and engineering career brochures (all disciplines), contact
Junior Engineering Technical Society (JETS)
1420 King Street, Suite 405
Alexandria, VA 22314-2794
Tel: 703-548-5387
Email: info@jets.org
http://www.jets.org

For a petroleum engineering career brochure, a list of petroleum engineering schools, and scholarship information, contact
Society of Petroleum Engineers
PO Box 833836
Richardson, TX 75083-3836
Tel: 972-952-9393
Email: spedal@spe.org
http://www.spe.org

For a Frontiers program brochure and application, contact
Worcester Polytechnic Institute
100 Institute Road
Worcester, MA 01609-2280
Tel: 508-831-5286
Email: frontiers@wpi.edu
http://www.admissions.wpi.edu/Frontiers

Quality Control Engineers

QUICK FACTS

School Subjects
Mathematics
Physics

Personal Skills
Mechanical/manipulative
Technical/scientific

Work Environment
Primarily indoors
Primarily one location

Minimum Education Level
Bachelor's degree

Salary Range
$46,300 to $75,580 to
$128,160+

Certification or Licensing
Voluntary

Outlook
More slowly than the average

DOT
012

GOE
05.01.04 (engineers)

NOC
2261

O*NET-SOC
N/A

OVERVIEW

Quality control engineers plan and direct procedures and activities that will ensure the quality of materials and goods. They select the best techniques for a specific process or method, determine the level of quality needed, and take the necessary action to maintain or improve quality performance.

HISTORY

Quality control technology is an outgrowth of the industrial revolution, which began in England in the 18th century. Each person involved in the manufacturing process was responsible for a particular part of the process. The worker's responsibility was further specialized by the introduction of the concept of interchangeable parts in the late 18th and early 19th centuries. In a manufacturing process using this concept, a worker concentrated on making just one component, while other workers concentrated on creating other components. Such specialization led to increased production efficiency, especially as manufacturing processes became mechanized during the early part of the 20th century. It also meant, however, that no one worker was responsible for the overall quality of the product. This led to the need for another kind of specialized production worker whose primary responsibility was not one aspect of the product but rather its overall quality.

This responsibility initially belonged to the mechanical engineers and technicians who developed the manufacturing systems, equip-

A quality control engineer gathers a sample for testing in a manufacturing plant. *(Corbis)*

ment, and procedures. After World War II, however, a new field emerged that was dedicated solely to quality control. Along with specially trained persons to test and inspect products coming off assembly lines, new instruments, equipment, and techniques were developed to measure and monitor specified standards.

At first, quality control engineers were primarily responsible for random checks of products to ensure they met all specifications. This usually entailed testing and inspecting either finished products or products at various stages of production.

During the 1980s, a quality movement spread across the United States. Faced with increased global competition, especially from Japanese manufacturers, many U.S. companies sought to improve quality and productivity. Quality improvement concepts such as Total Quality Management (TQM), Six Sigma, continuous improvement, quality circles, and zero defects gained popularity and changed the way companies viewed quality and quality control practices. A new philosophy emerged, emphasizing quality as the concern of all individuals involved in producing goods and directing that quality be monitored at all stages of manufacturing, not just at the end of production or at random stages of manufacturing.

Today, most companies focus on improving quality during all stages of production, with an emphasis on preventing defects rather than merely identifying defective parts. There is an increased use of sophisticated automated equipment that can test and inspect products as they are manufactured. Automated equipment includes cameras, X rays, lasers, scanners, metal detectors, video inspection systems, electronic sensors, and machine vision systems that can detect the slightest flaw or variance from accepted tolerances. Many companies use statistical process control to record levels of quality and determine the best manufacturing and quality procedures. Quality control engineers work with employees from all departments of a company to train them in the best quality methods and to seek improvements to manufacturing processes to further improve quality levels.

Many companies today are seeking to conform to international standards for quality, such as ISO 9000, in order to compete with foreign companies and to sell products to companies in countries around the world. These standards are based on concepts of quality of industrial goods and services and involve documenting quality methods and procedures.

THE JOB

Quality control engineers are responsible for developing, implementing, and directing processes and practices that result in a desired level of quality for manufactured parts. They identify standards to measure the quality of a part or product, analyze factors that affect quality, and determine the best practices to ensure quality.

Quality control engineers set up procedures to monitor and control quality, devise methods to improve quality, and analyze quality control methods for effectiveness, productivity, and cost factors. They are involved in all aspects of quality during a product's life cycle. Not only do they focus on ensuring quality during production operations, they also get involved in product design and product evaluation. Quality control engineers may be specialists who work with engineers and industrial designers during the design phase of a product, or they may work with sales and marketing professionals to evaluate reports from consumers on how well a product is performing. Quality control engineers are responsible for ensuring that all incoming materials used in a finished product meet required standards and that all instruments and automated equipment used to test and monitor parts during production perform properly. They supervise and direct workers involved in assuring quality, including quality control technicians, inspectors, and related production personnel.

REQUIREMENTS

High School

To prepare for this career, you should take high school classes in mathematics (including algebra, geometry, and statistics), physical sciences, physics, and chemistry. You should also take shop, mechanical drawing, and computer courses. In addition, you should take English courses that develop your reading skills, your ability to write well-organized reports with a logical development of ideas, and your ability to speak comfortably and effectively in front of a group.

Postsecondary Training

Quality control engineers generally have a bachelor's degree in engineering. Many quality control engineers receive degrees in industrial or manufacturing engineering. Some receive degrees in metallurgical, mechanical, electrical, chemical engineering, or business administration, depending on where they plan to work. College engineering programs vary based on the type of engineering program. Most programs take four to five years to complete and include courses in mathematics, physics, and chemistry. Other useful courses include statistics, logistics, business management, and technical writing.

Certification or Licensing

Although there are no licensing or certification requirements designed specifically for quality control engineers, some need to meet special requirements that apply only within the industry employing them. Many quality control engineers pursue voluntary certification from professional organizations to indicate that they have achieved a certain level of expertise. The American Society for Quality (ASQ), for example, offers certification at a number of levels including quality engineer certification and software quality engineer. Requirements include having a certain amount of work experience, having proof of professionalism (such as being a licensed professional engineer), and passing a written examination.

Many employers value this certification and take it into consideration when making new hires or giving promotions.

Other Requirements

Quality control engineers need scientific and mathematical aptitudes, strong interpersonal skills, and leadership abilities. Good judgment is also needed, as quality control engineers must weigh all the factors influencing quality and determine procedures that incorporate price, performance, and cost factors.

EXPLORING

Quality control engineers work with scientific instruments; therefore, you should take academic or industrial arts courses that introduce you to different kinds of scientific or technical equipment. You should also take electrical and machine shop courses, mechanical drawing courses, and chemistry courses with lab sections. Joining a radio, computer, or science club is also a good way to gain experience and to engage in team-building and problem-solving activities. Active participation in clubs is a good way to learn skills that will benefit you when working with other professionals in manufacturing and industrial settings. To find out more about engineering in general, join the Junior Engineering Technical Society (JETS), which will give you the opportunity to test your skills and meet professionals and others interested in engineering, math, and science. (Visit the JETS Web site at http://www.jets.org.)

You should keep in mind that quality control activities and quality control professionals are often directly involved with manufacturing processes. If it is at all possible, try to get a part-time or summer job in a manufacturing setting, even if you are not specifically in the quality control area. Although your work may mean doing menial tasks, it will give you firsthand experience in the environment and demonstrate the depth of your interest to future employers.

EMPLOYERS

There are approximately 160,000 industrial production managers (a group that includes quality control engineers) working in the United States. The majority of quality control engineers are employed in the manufacturing sector of the economy. Because engineers work in all areas of industry, their employers vary widely in size, product, location, and prestige.

STARTING OUT

Quality control engineers can learn of job openings through their schools' career services office, recruiters, and job fairs. In many cases, employers prefer to hire engineers who have some work experience in their particular industry. For this reason, applicants who have had summer or part-time employment or participated in a work-study or internship program have greater job opportunities.

Students may also learn about openings through help wanted ads or by using the services of state and private employment services. They also may apply directly to companies that employ quality control engineers. Students can identify and research such companies by using job resource guides and other reference materials available at most public libraries.

ADVANCEMENT

Quality control engineers may have limited opportunities to advance within their companies. However, because quality control engineers work in all areas of industry, they have the opportunity to change jobs or companies to pursue more challenging or higher paying positions. Quality control engineers who work in companies with large staffs of quality personnel can become quality control directors or advance to operations management positions.

EARNINGS

Earnings vary according to the type of work, the industry, and the geographical location. Quality control engineers earn salaries comparable to other engineers. According to the U.S. Department of Labor, the median yearly income for industrial production managers was $75,580 in 2005. The lowest paid 10 percent earned less than $46,300, and the highest paid 10 percent made more than $128,160.

Most companies offer benefits that include paid vacations, paid holidays, and health insurance. Actual benefits depend on the company but may also include pension plans, profit sharing, 401(k) plans, and tuition assistance programs.

WORK ENVIRONMENT

Quality control engineers work in a variety of settings, and their conditions of work vary accordingly. Most work in manufacturing plants, though the type of industry determines the actual environment. For example, quality control engineers in the metals industry usually work in foundries or iron and steel plants. Conditions are hot, dirty, and noisy. Other factories, such as for the electronics or pharmaceutical industries, are generally quiet and clean. Most engineers have offices separate from the production floor, but they still need to spend a fair amount of time there. Engineers involved with testing and product analysis work in comfortable surroundings, such as a laboratory or workshop. Even in these settings, however, they may be exposed to unpleasant fumes and toxic chemicals. In general, quality control engineers work inside and are expected to do some light lifting and carrying (usually not more than 20 pounds). Because many manufacturing plants operate 24 hours a day, some quality control professionals may need to work second or third shifts.

As with most engineering positions, the work can be both challenging and routine. Engineers can expect to find some tasks repetitious and tedious. In most cases, though, the work provides variety and satisfaction from using highly developed skills and technical expertise.

OUTLOOK

The employment outlook for quality control engineers depends, to some degree, on general economic conditions. The U.S. Department of Labor projects slower-than-average growth for the field of industrial production management, which includes quality control engineers. This is a result of increased productivity as a result of better technology, in addition to a greater reliance on manufacturing workers to constantly monitor the quality of their own work. However, the role of the quality control engineer is vital to production and cannot be eliminated. Thus, there will still be new jobs to replace people retiring from or otherwise leaving this field.

Many companies are making vigorous efforts to make their manufacturing processes more efficient, lower costs, and improve productivity and quality. Opportunities for quality control engineers should be good in the food and beverage industries, pharmaceutical firms, electronics companies, and chemical companies. Quality control engineers also may find employment in industries using robotics equipment or in the aerospace, biomedical, bioengineering, environmental controls, and transportation industries. Lowered rates of manufacturing in the automotive industry will decrease the number of quality control personnel needed for these areas. Declines in employment in some industries may occur because of the increased use of automated equipment that tests and inspects parts during production operations.

FOR MORE INFORMATION

For information on certification and student chapters, contact
American Society for Quality
600 North Plankinton Avenue
Milwaukee, WI 53203-2914
Tel: 800-248-1946
Email: help@asq.org
http://www.asq.org

ASTM International offers seminars and other training programs for those involved in testing materials and quality assurance. Visit its Web site to read articles from its magazine Standardization News.
ASTM International
100 Barr Harbor Drive
PO Box C700
West Conshohocken, PA 19428-2959
Tel: 610-832-9585
http://www.astm.org

Robotics Engineers

OVERVIEW

Robotics engineers design, develop, build, and program robots and robotic devices; including peripheral equipment and computer software used to control robots. Robots are used widely in the aerospace industry for space exploration and to assist in the manufacturing of aircraft and spacecraft.

HISTORY

Robots are devices that perform tasks ordinarily performed by humans; they seem to operate with an almost-human intelligence. The idea of robots can be traced back to the ancient Greek and Egyptian civilizations. An inventor from the first century A.D., Hero of Alexandria, invented a machine that would automatically open the doors of a temple when the priest lit a fire in the altar. During the later periods of the Middle Ages, the Renaissance, and the 17th and 18th centuries, interest in robot-like mechanisms turned mostly to automatons, devices that imitate human and animal appearance and activity but perform no useful task.

The industrial revolution inspired the invention of many different kinds of automatic machinery. One of the most important robotics inventions occurred in 1804: Joseph-Marie Jacquard's method for controlling machinery by means of a programmed set of instructions recorded on a punched paper tape that was fed into a machine to direct its movements.

The word *robot* and the concepts associated with it were first introduced in the early 1920s. They made their appearance in a play titled *R.U.R.*, which stands for Rossum's Universal Robots, written by Czechoslovakian dramatist Karel Capek. The play involves human-like robotic machines created to perform manual tasks for their human masters.

During the 1950s and 1960s, advances in the fields of automation and computer science led to the development of experimental robots that could imitate a wide range of human activity, including self-regulated and self-propelled movement (either on wheels or on legs), the ability to sense and manipulate objects, and the ability to select a course of action on the basis of conditions around them.

In 1954, George Devol designed the first programmable robot in the United States. He named it the Universal Automation, which was later shortened to Unimation, which also became the name of the first robot company. Hydraulic robots, controlled by numerical control programming, were developed in the 1960s and were used initially by the automobile industry in assembly line operations. By 1973, robots were being built with electric power and electronic controls, which allowed greater flexibility and increased uses.

Robotic technology has evolved significantly in the past few decades. Early robotic equipment, often referred to as first-generation robots, were simple mechanical arms or devices that could perform precise, repetitive motions at high speeds. They contained no artificial intelligence capabilities. Second-generation robots, which came into use in the 1980s, are controlled by minicomputers and programmed by computer language. They contain sensors, such as vision systems and pressure, proximity, and tactile sensors, which provide information about the outside environment. Third-generation robots, also controlled by minicomputers and equipped with sensory devices, are currently being developed. Referred to as "smart" robots, they can work on their own without supervision by an external computer or human being.

The evolution of robots is closely tied to the study of human anatomy and movement of the human body. The early robots were modeled after arms, then wrists. Second-generation robots include features that model human hands. Third-generation robots are being developed with legs and complex joint technology. They also incorporate multisensory input controls, such as ultrasonic sensors or sensors that can "sniff" and "taste."

THE JOB

The majority of robotics engineers work within the field of computer-integrated manufacturing or programmable automation. Using computer science technology, engineers design and develop robots and other automated equipment, including computer software used to program robots.

The title robotics engineer may be used to refer to any engineer who works primarily with robots. Oftentimes, their educational background lies within the many engineering specialties—mechanical, electrical, computer, or manufacturing. There has been, in recent times, a growing number of engineering professionals graduating with a degree in robotics engineering.

Robotics engineers have a thorough understanding of robotic systems and equipment and know the different technologies available to create robots for specific applications. They have a strong foundation in computer systems and how computers are linked to robots. They also have an understanding of manufacturing production requirements and how robots can best be used in automated systems to achieve cost efficiency, productivity, and quality. Robotics engineers may analyze and evaluate a manufacturer's operating system to determine whether robots can be used efficiently instead of other automated equipment or humans.

Many other types of engineers are also involved in the design, development, fabrication, programming, and operation of robots. Following are brief descriptions of these types of engineers and how they relate to robotics.

Electrical and electronics engineers research, design, and develop the electrical systems used in robots and the power supply, if it is electrical. These engineers may specialize in areas such as integrated circuit theory, lasers, electronic sensors, optical components, and energy power systems.

Mechanical engineers are involved in the design, fabrication, and operation of the mechanical systems of a robot. These engineers need a strong working knowledge of mechanical components such as gripper mechanisms, bearings, gears, chains, belts, and actuators. Some robots are controlled by pneumatic or mechanical power supplies, and these engineers need to be specialists in designing these systems. Mechanical engineers also select the material used to make robots. They test robots once they are constructed.

Computer engineers design the computer systems that are used to program robots. Sometimes these systems are built into a robot and other times they are a part of separate equipment that is used to control robots. Some computer engineers also write computer programs.

Industrial engineers are specialists in manufacturing operations. They determine the physical layout of a factory to best utilize production equipment. They may determine the placement of robotic equipment. They also are responsible for safety rules and practices and for ensuring that robotic equipment is used properly.

CAD/CAM engineers (computer-aided design/computer-aided manufacturing) are experts in automated production processes. They design and supervise manufacturing systems that utilize robots and other automated equipment.

Manufacturing engineers manage the entire production process. They may evaluate production operations to determine whether robots can be used in an assembly line and make recommendations on purchasing robotic equipment. Some manufacturing engineers design robots. Other engineers specialize in a specific area of robotics, such as artificial intelligence, vision systems, and sensor systems. These specialists are developing robots with "brains" that are similar to those of humans.

REQUIREMENTS

High School

In high school, you should take as many science, math, and computer classes as possible. Recommended courses include biology, chemistry, physics, algebra, trigonometry, geometry, calculus, graphics, computer science, English, speech, composition, social studies, and drafting. In addition, take shop and vocational classes that teach blueprint and electrical schematic reading, the use of hand tools, drafting, and the basics of electricity and electronics.

Postsecondary Training

Because changes occur so rapidly within this field, it is recommended that engineers get a broad-based education that encompasses robotics but does not focus solely on robotics. Programs that provide the widest career base are those in automated manufacturing, which includes robotics, electronics, and computer science.

In order to become an engineer it is necessary to earn a bachelor of science degree, which generally takes four or five years to complete. More than 400 colleges and universities offer courses in robotics or related technology. Many different types of programs are available. Some colleges and universities offer robotics engineering degrees and others offer engineering degrees with concentrations or options in robotics and manufacturing engineering. For some higher-level jobs, such as robotics designer, a master of science or doctoral degree is required. Carnegie Mellon University has an extensive robotics program and offers an undergraduate minor, as well as master's and doctoral degrees in robotics. Visit http://robotics.nasa.gov/students/

robo_u.php for a list of colleges and universities that offer educational programs in robotics.

Other Requirements

Because the field of robotics is rapidly changing, one of the most important requirements for a person interested in a career in robotics is the willingness to pursue additional training on an ongoing basis during his or her career. After completing their formal education, engineers may need to take additional classes in a college or university or take advantage of training offered through their employers and professional associations.

Robotics engineers need manual dexterity, good hand-eye coordination, and mechanical and electrical aptitude.

EXPLORING

Because robotics is a relatively new field, it is important to learn as much as possible about current trends and recent technologies. Reading books and articles in trade magazines provides an excellent way to learn about what is happening in robotics technologies and expected future trends. Trade magazines with informative articles include *Robotics Engineering, Robotics and Autonomous Systems,* and *Unmanned Systems.*

You can become a robot hobbyist and build your own robots or buy toy robots and experiment with them. Complete robot kits are available through a number of companies and range from simple, inexpensive robots to highly complex robots with advanced features and accessories. A number of books that give instructions and helpful hints on building robots can be found at most public libraries and bookstores. In addition, relatively inexpensive and simple toy robots are available from electronics shops, department stores, and mail order companies.

You can also participate in competitions. The International Aerial Robotics Competition is sponsored by the Association for Unmanned Vehicle Systems International. This competition, which requires teams of students to build complex robots, is open to college students. Visit http://avdil.gtri.gatech.edu/AUVS/IARCLaunchPoint.html for more information.

Participating in summer camps is another great way to explore the field. Visit http://robotics.nasa.gov/students/camp.php to learn more about camps offered by NASA and other organizations.

Another great way to learn about robotics is to attend trade shows. Many robotics and automated machinery manufacturers exhibit their products at shows and conventions. Numerous such trade shows are held every year in different parts of the country. Information about these trade shows is available through association trade magazines and periodicals such as *Managing Automation* (http://www.managingautomation.com).

Other activities that foster knowledge and skills relevant to a career in robotics include membership in high school science clubs, participation in science fairs, and pursuing hobbies that involve electronics, mechanical equipment, and model building.

EMPLOYERS

Robotics engineers are employed in virtually every manufacturing industry. A large number of robotics manufacturers are found in California, Michigan, Illinois, Indiana, Pennsylvania, Ohio, Connecticut, Texas, British Columbia, and Ontario, although companies exist in many other states and parts of Canada. Government agencies also employ a significant number of robotics engineers. With the trend toward automation continuing—often via the use of robots—people trained in robotics can expect to find employment with almost all types of manufacturing companies, as well as many government agencies, in the future.

STARTING OUT

Graduates of robotics engineering programs may learn about available openings through their schools' career services office. It also may be possible to learn about job openings through want ads in newspapers and trade magazines and job fairs.

In many cases, it will be necessary to research companies that manufacture or use robots and apply directly to them. The organizations listed at the end of this article may offer publications with classified ads, or other job search information.

Job opportunities may be good at small start-up companies or a start-up robotics unit of a large company. Many times these employers are willing to hire inexperienced workers as apprentices or assistants. Then, when their sales and production grow, these workers have the best chances for advancement.

ADVANCEMENT

Engineers may start as part of an engineering team and do relatively simple tasks under the supervision of a project manager or more experienced engineer. With experience and demonstrated competency, they can move into higher engineering positions. Engineers who demonstrate good interpersonal skills, leadership abilities, and technical expertise may become team leaders, project managers, or chief engineers. Engineers can also move into supervisory or management positions. Some engineers pursue an M.B.A. (master of business administration) degree. These engineers are able to move into top management positions. Some engineers also develop specialties, such as artificial intelligence, and move into highly specialized engineering positions.

Experienced engineers may teach courses at their workplace or find teaching opportunities at a local school or community college.

Other routes for advancement include becoming a sales representative for a robotics manufacturing or design firm or working as an independent contractor for companies that use or manufacture robots.

EARNINGS

Earnings and benefits vary widely based on the size of the company, geographic location, nature of the production process, and complexity of the robots. In general, engineers with a bachelor of science degree earn annual salaries between $50,000 and $52,000 in their first job after graduation. According to the U.S. Department of Labor, mechanical engineers earned median annual salaries of $67,590 in 2005. Median annual earnings of computer hardware engineers were $84,420, and median annual earnings of electronics engineers, except computer were $78,030. All of these engineers can earn annual salaries well over $100,000 with increased experience and responsibility.

Employers offer a variety of benefits that can include the following: paid holidays, vacations, personal days, and sick leave; medical, dental, disability, and life insurance; 401(k) plans, pension and retirement plans; profit sharing; and educational assistance programs.

WORK ENVIRONMENT

Robotics engineers may work either for a company that manufactures robots or a company or government organization that uses robots. Most companies that manufacture robots are relatively clean, quiet, and comfortable environments. Engineers may work in an office or on the production floor.

Engineers who work in a company that uses robots may work in noisy, hot, and dirty surroundings. Others may work in clean, well lighted offices or control rooms. Conditions vary based on the type of industry within which one works. Some robotics personnel are required

Books to Read

Cook, David. *Robot Building for Beginners*. Berkeley, Calif.: Apress, 2002.

Gurstelle, William. *Building Bots: Designing and Building Warrior Robots*. Chicago: Chicago Review Press, 2002.

Hambley, Allan R. *Electrical Engineering: Principles and Applications*. 4th ed. Upper Saddle River, N.J.: Prentice Hall, 2007.

Iovine, John. *Robots, Androids, and Animatrons: 12 Incredible Projects You Can Build*. 2d ed. New York: McGraw-Hill/TAB Electronics, 2001.

McComb, Gordon. *Robot Builder's Sourcebook: Over 2,500 Sources for Robotic Parts*. New York: McGraw-Hill/TAB Electronics, 2002.

Miller, Rex, and Mark R. Miller. *Electronics the Easy Way*. 4th ed. Hauppauge, N.Y.: Barron's Educational Series, 2002.

Williams, Karl. *Build Your Own Humanoid Robots: 6 Amazing and Affordable Projects*. New York: McGraw-Hill/TAB Electronics, 2004.

to work in clean room environments, which keep electronic components free of dirt and other contaminants. Workers in these environments wear facemasks, hair coverings, and special protective clothing.

Some engineers may confront potentially hazardous conditions in the workplace. Robots, after all, are often designed and used precisely because the task they perform involves some risk to humans: handling laser beams, arc-welding equipment, radioactive substances, or hazardous chemicals. When they design, test, build, install, and repair robots, it is inevitable that some engineers will be exposed to these same risks. Plant safety procedures protect the attentive and cautious worker, but carelessness in such settings can be especially dangerous.

In general, most engineers work 40-hour workweeks, although overtime may be required for special projects or to repair equipment that is shutting down a production line.

OUTLOOK

Employment opportunities for robotics engineers are closely tied to economic conditions in the United States and in the global marketplace. The U.S. Department of Labor predicts the fields of mechanical, electronics, and computer hardware engineering will grow about as fast as the average through 2014, mainly due to increased foreign competition. Competition for engineering jobs will be stiff, and opportunities will be best for those that have advanced degrees.

FOR MORE INFORMATION

For information on competitions and student membership, contact
Association for Unmanned Vehicle Systems International
2700 South Quincy Street, Suite 400
Arlington, VA 22206-2226
Tel: 703-845-9671
Email: info@auvsi.org
http://www.auvsi.org

For career information, company profiles, training seminars, and educational resources, contact
Robotic Industries Association
900 Victors Way, Suite 140
PO Box 3724
Ann Arbor, MI 48106-2735
Tel: 734-994-6088
http://www.roboticsonline.com

For information on careers and educational programs, contact
Robotics and Automation Society
Institute of Electrical and Electronics Engineers
445 Hoes Lane
Piscataway, NJ 08855-4141
http://www.ieee-ras.org

For information on educational programs, competitions, and student membership in the SME, contact
Society of Manufacturing Engineers (SME)
One SME Drive
Dearborn, MI 48121-2408
Tel: 800-733-4763
Email: service@sme.org
http://www.sme.org

Visit the following Web site for information on robotics education and summer camps and programs.
The Robotics Alliance Project
National Aeronautics and Space Administration
http://robotics.nasa.gov

Software Engineers

OVERVIEW

Software engineers are responsible for customizing existing software programs to meet the needs and desires of a particular business or industry. First, they spend considerable time researching, defining, and analyzing the problem at hand. Then, they develop software programs to resolve the problem on the computer. There are approximately 800,000 computer software engineers employed in the United States.

HISTORY

Advances in computer technology have enabled professionals to put computers to work in a range of activities once thought impossible. In the past several years, software engineers have been able to take advantage of computer hardware improvements in speed, memory capacity, reliability, and accuracy to create programs that do just about anything. Computer engineering blossomed as a distinct subfield in the computer industry after the new performance levels were achieved. This relative lateness is explained by the fact that the programs written by software engineers to solve business and scientific problems are very intricate and complex, requiring a lot of computing power. Although many computer scientists will continue to focus their research on further developing hardware, the emphasis in the field has moved more squarely to software, and the U.S. Department of Labor predicts that software engineers will be among the fastest growing occupations in the United States through the next decade.

THE JOB

Every day, businesses, scientists, and government agencies encounter difficult problems that they cannot solve manually, either because the problem is just too complicated or because it would take too much time to calculate the appropriate solutions. For example, astronomers receive thousands of pieces of data every hour from probes and satellites in space as well as telescopes here on Earth. If they had to process the information themselves, compile careful comparisons with previous years' readings, look for patterns or cycles, and keep accurate records of the origin of the various data, it would be so cumbersome and lengthy a project as to make it next to impossible. They can, however, process the data with the extensive help of computers. Computer software engineers define and analyze specific problems in business or science and help develop computer software applications that effectively solve them. The software engineers who work in the field of astronomy are well versed in its concepts, but many other kinds of software engineers exist as well.

Software engineers fall into two basic categories. *Systems software engineers* build and maintain entire computer systems for a company. *Applications software engineers* design, create, and modify general computer applications software or specialized utility programs.

Engineers who work on computer systems research how a company's departments and their respective computer systems are organized. For example, there might be customer service, ordering, inventory, billing, shipping, and payroll record-keeping departments. Systems software engineers suggest ways to coordinate all these parts. They might set up intranets or networks that link computers within the organization and ease communication.

Some applications software engineers develop packaged software applications, such as word processing, graphic design, or database programs, for software development companies. Other applications engineers design customized software for individual businesses or organizations. For example, a software engineer might work with an insurance company to develop new ways to reduce paperwork, such as claim forms, applications, and bill processing. Applications engineers write programs using programming languages like C++ and Java.

Software engineers sometimes specialize in a particular industry such as the chemical industry, insurance, or medicine, which requires knowledge of that industry in addition to computer expertise. Some engineers work for consulting firms that complete software projects for different clients on an individual basis. Others work for large companies that hire full-time engineers to develop software customized to their needs.

Software engineering technicians assist engineers in completing projects. They are usually knowledgeable in analog, digital, and microprocessor electronics and programming techniques. Technicians know enough about program design and computer languages to fill in details left out by engineers or programmers, who conceive of the program from a large-scale perspective. Technicians might also test new software applications with special diagnostic equipment.

Both systems and applications software engineering involve extremely detail-oriented work. Since computers do only what they are programmed to do, engineers have to account for every bit of information with a programming command. Software engineers are thus required to be very well organized and precise. In order to achieve this, they generally follow strict procedures in completing an assignment.

First, they interview clients and colleagues to determine exactly what they want the final program to accomplish. Defining the problem by outlining the goal can sometimes be difficult, especially when clients have little technical training. Then, engineers evaluate the software applications already in use by the client to understand how and why they are failing to fulfill the needs of the operation. After this period of fact gathering, the engineers use methods of scientific analysis and mathematical models to develop possible solutions to the problems. These analytical methods help them predict and measure the outcomes of different proposed designs.

When they have developed a clear idea of what type of program is required to fulfill the client's needs, they draw up a detailed proposal that includes estimates of time and cost allocations. Management must then decide if the project will meet their needs, is a good investment, and whether or not it will be undertaken.

Once a proposal is accepted, both software engineers and technicians begin work on the project. They verify with hardware engineers that the proposed software program can be completed with existing hardware systems. Typically, the engineer writes program specifications and the technician uses his or her knowledge of computer languages to write preliminary programming. Engineers focus most of their effort on program strategies, testing procedures, and reviewing technicians' work.

Software engineers are usually responsible for a significant amount of technical writing, including project proposals, progress reports, and user manuals. They are required to meet regularly with clients to keep project goals clear and learn about any changes as quickly as possible.

When the program is completed, the software engineer organizes a demonstration of the final product to the client. Supervisors, management, and users are generally present. Some software engineers may offer to install the program, train users on it, and make arrangements for ongoing technical support.

REQUIREMENTS
High School
A bachelor's or advanced degree in computer science or engineering is required for most software engineers. Thus, to prepare for college studies while in high school, take as many computer, math, and science courses as possible; they provide fundamental math and computer knowledge and teach analytical thinking skills. Classes that rely on schematic drawing and flowcharts are also very valuable. English and speech courses will help you improve your communication skills, which are very important for software engineers.

Postsecondary Training
As more and more well-educated professionals enter the industry, most employers now require a bachelor's degree. A typical degree concentration for an applications software engineer is software engineering or computer science. Systems software engineers typically pursue a concentration in computer science or computer information systems.

Obtaining a postsecondary degree is usually considered challenging and even difficult. In addition to natural ability, you should be hard working and determined to succeed. If you plan to work in a specific technical field, such as medicine, law, or business, you should receive some formal training in that particular discipline.

Certification or Licensing
Software engineers often pursue commercial certification. These programs are usually run by computer companies that wish to train professionals to work with their products. Classes are challenging and examinations can be rigorous. New programs are introduced every year.

Other Requirements
As a software engineer, you will need strong communications skills in order to be able to make formal business presentations and interact with people having different levels of computer expertise. You must also be detail oriented and work well under pressure.

EXPLORING

Try to spend a day with a working software engineer in order to experience firsthand what their job is like. School guidance counselors can help you arrange such a visit. You can also talk to your high school computer teacher for more information.

In general, you should be intent on learning as much as possible about computers and computer software. You should learn about new developments by reading trade magazines and talking to other computer users. You also can join computer clubs and surf the Internet for information about working in this field.

EMPLOYERS

About 800,000 computer software engineers are employed in the United States. Approximately 460,000 work with applications and 340,000 work with systems software. Software engineering is done in many fields, including medical, industrial, military, communications, aerospace, scientific, and other commercial businesses. Almost 30 percent of software engineers—the largest concentration in the field—work in computer systems design and related services.

STARTING OUT

As a technical, vocational, or university student of software engineering, you should work closely with your schools' career services office, as many professionals find their first position through on-campus recruiting. Career services office staff are well trained to provide tips on resume writing, interviewing techniques, and locating job leads.

Individuals not working with a school career services office can check the classified ads for job openings. They also can work with a local employment agency that places computer professionals in appropriate jobs. Many openings in the computer industry are publicized by word of mouth, so you should stay in touch with working computer professionals to learn who is hiring. In addition, these people may be willing to refer you directly to the person in charge of recruiting.

ADVANCEMENT

Software engineers who demonstrate leadership qualities and thorough technical know-how may become *project team leaders* who are responsible for full-scale software development projects. Project team leaders oversee the work of technicians and engineers. They determine the overall parameters of a project, calculate time schedules and financial budgets, divide the project into smaller tasks, and assign these tasks to engineers. Overall, they do both managerial and technical work.

Software engineers with experience as project team leaders may be promoted to a position as *software manager,* running a large research and development department. Managers oversee software projects with a more encompassing perspective; they help choose projects to be undertaken, select project team leaders and engineering teams, and assign individual projects. In some cases, they may be required to travel, solicit new business, and contribute to the general marketing strategy of the company.

Many computer professionals find that their interests change over time. As long as individuals are well qualified and keep up to date with the latest technology, they are usually able to find positions in other areas of the computer industry.

EARNINGS

Computer software engineers with a bachelor's degree in computer engineering earned starting salaries of $52,464 in 2005, according to the National Association of Colleges and Employers. New computer engineers with a master's degree averaged $60,354. Computer engineers specializing in applications earned median annual salaries of $77,090 in 2005, according to the U.S. Department of Labor. The lowest 10 percent averaged less than $47,370, and the highest 10 percent earned $116,150 or more annually. Software engineers specializing in systems software earned median salaries of $82,120 in 2005. The lowest paid 10 percent averaged $51,890 annually, and the highest paid engineers made $120,410 per year. Experienced software engineers can earn over $150,000 a year. When software engineers are promoted to project team leader or software manager, they earn even more. Software engineers generally earn more in geographical areas where there are clusters of computer companies, such as the Silicon Valley in Northern California.

Most software engineers work for companies that offer extensive benefits, including health insurance, sick leave, and paid vacation. In some smaller computer companies, however, benefits may be limited.

WORK ENVIRONMENT

Software engineers usually work in comfortable office environments. Overall, they usually work 40-hour weeks, but this depends on the nature of the employer and expertise of the engineer. In consulting firms, for example, it is typical for engineers to work long hours and frequently travel to out-of-town assignments.

Software engineers generally receive an assignment and a time frame within which to accomplish it; daily work details are often left up to the individuals. Some engineers work relatively lightly at the beginning of a project, but work a lot of overtime at the end in order to catch up. Most engineers are not compensated for overtime. Software engineering can be stressful, especially when engineers must work to meet deadlines. Working with programming languages and intense details is often frustrating. Therefore, software engineers should be patient, enjoy problem-solving challenges, and work well under pressure.

OUTLOOK

The field of software engineering is expected to be one of the fastest growing occupations through 2014, according to the U.S. Department of Labor. Demands made on computers increase everyday and from all industries. Rapid growth in the computer systems design and related industries will account for much of this growth. In addition, businesses will continue to implement new and innovative technology to remain competitive, and they will need software engineers to do this. Software engineers will also be needed to handle ever-growing capabilities of computer networks, e-commerce, and wireless technologies, as well as the security features needed to protect such systems from outside attacks. Outsourcing of jobs in this field to foreign countries will temper growth somewhat, but overall the future of software engineering is very bright.

Since technology changes so rapidly, software engineers are advised to keep up on the latest developments. While the need for software engineers will remain high, computer languages will probably change every few years and software engineers will need to attend seminars and workshops to learn new computer languages and software design. They also should read trade magazines, surf the Internet, and talk with colleagues about the field. These kinds of continuing education techniques help ensure that software engineers are best equipped to meet the needs of the workplace.

FOR MORE INFORMATION

For information on internships, student membership, and the student magazine Crossroads, *contact*

Association for Computing Machinery
Two Penn Plaza, Suite 701

New York, NY 10121-0701
Tel: 800-342-6626
http://www.acm.org

For certification information, contact
Institute for Certification of Computing Professionals
2350 East Devon Avenue, Suite 115
Des Plaines, IL 60018-4610
Tel: 800-843-8227
http://www.iccp.org

For information on scholarships, student membership, and the student newsletter, looking.forward, *contact*
IEEE Computer Society
1730 Massachusetts Avenue, NW
Washington, DC 20036-1992
Tel: 202-371-0101
http://www.computer.org

For more information on careers in computer software, contact
Software & Information Industry Association
1090 Vermont Avenue, NW, Sixth Floor
Washington, DC 20005-4095
Tel: 202-289-7442
http://www.siia.net

Transportation Engineers

OVERVIEW

Transportation engineers study factors that influence traffic conditions on roads and streets, including street lighting, visibility and location of signs and signals, entrances and exits, and the presence of factories or shopping malls. They use this information to design and implement plans and electronic systems that improve the flow of traffic. There are approximately 24,000 transportation engineers in the United States.

HISTORY

During the early colonial days, dirt roads and Native American trails were the primary means of land travel. In 1806, the U.S. Congress provided for the construction of the first road, known as the Cumberland Road. More and more roads were built, connecting neighborhoods, towns, cities, and states. As the population increased and modes of travel began to advance, more roads were needed to facilitate commerce, tourism, and daily transportation. Electric traffic signals were introduced in the United States in 1928 to help control automobile traffic. Because land travel was becoming increasingly complex, transportation engineers were trained to ensure safe travel on roads and highways, in detours and construction work zones, and for special events such as sports competitions and presidential conventions, among others.

THE JOB

Transportation engineers study factors such as signal timing, traffic flow, high-accident zones, lighting, road capacity, and entrances and exits in order to increase traffic safety and to improve the flow of traffic. In planning and creating their designs, engineers may observe such general traffic influences as the proximity of shopping malls, railroads, airports, or factories, and other factors that affect how well traffic moves. They apply standardized mathematical formulas to certain measurements to compute traffic signal duration and speed limits, and they prepare drawings showing the location of new signals or other traffic control devices. They may perform statistical studies of traffic conditions, flow, and volume, and they may—on the basis of such studies—recommend changes in traffic controls and regulations. Transportation engineers design improvement plans with the use of computers and through on-site investigation.

Transportation engineers address a variety of problems in their daily work. They may conduct studies and implement plans to reduce the number of accidents on a particularly dangerous section of highway. They might be asked to prepare traffic impact studies for new residential or industrial developments, implementing improvements to manage the increased flow of traffic. To do this, they may analyze and adjust the timing of traffic signals, suggest the widening of lanes, or recommend the introduction of bus or carpool lanes. In the performance of their duties, transportation engineers must be constantly aware of the effect their designs will have on nearby pedestrian traffic and on environmental concerns, such as air quality, noise pollution, and the presence of wetlands and other protected areas.

Transportation engineers use computers to monitor traffic flow onto highways and at intersections, to study frequent accident sites, to determine road and highway capacities, and to control and regulate the operation of traffic signals throughout entire cities. Computers allow transportation engineers to experiment with multiple design plans while monitoring cost, impact, and efficiency of a particular project.

Transportation engineers who work in government often design or oversee roads or entire public transportation systems. They might oversee the design, planning, and construction of new roads and highways or manage a system that controls the traffic signals by the use of a computer. Engineers frequently interact with a wide variety of people, from average citizens to business leaders and elected officials.

Transportation technicians assist transportation engineers. They collect data in the field by interviewing motorists at intersections where traffic is often congested or where an unusual number of accidents have occurred. They also use radar equipment or timing devices to determine the speed of passing vehicles at certain locations, and they use stopwatches to time traffic signals and other delays to traffic. Some transportation technicians may also have limited design duties.

REQUIREMENTS

High School

For a career in transportation engineering you need mathematical skills in algebra, logic, and geometry and a good working knowledge of statistics. You should have language skills that will enable you to write extensive reports making use of statistical data, and you should be able to present such reports before groups of people. You should also be familiar with computers and electronics in general. You need a basic understanding of the workings of government since you must frequently address regulations and zoning laws and meet and work with government officials. A high school diploma is the minimum educational requirement for transportation technicians.

Postsecondary Training

Transportation engineers must have a bachelor's degree in civil, electrical, mechanical, or chemical engineering. Because the field of transportation is so vast, many engineers have educational backgrounds in science, planning, computers, environmental planning, and other related fields. Educational courses for transportation engineers may include transportation planning, transportation engineering, highway design, and related courses such as computer science, urban planning, statistics, geography, business management, public administration, and economics.

Transportation engineers acquire some of their skills through on-the-job experience and training conferences and mini-courses offered by their employers, educational facilities, and professional engineering societies. Transportation technicians receive much of their training on the job and through education courses offered by various engineering organizations.

Certification or Licensing

The Institute of Transportation Engineers (ITE) offers certification as a professional traffic operations engineer. To become certified, you must have at least four years of professional practice in traffic operations engineering; hold a valid license to practice civil, mechanical, electrical or general professional engineering; and pass an examination.

Engineers whose work may affect the life, health, or safety of the public must be registered according to regulations in all 50 states and the District of Columbia. Applicants for registration must have received a degree from an Accreditation Board for Engineering and Technology-accredited engineering program and have four years of experience. They must also pass a written examination administered by the state in which they plan to work. For more information on licensing and examination requirements, visit http://www.ncees.org.

Other Requirements

Transportation engineers should enjoy the challenge of solving problems. You should have good oral and written communication skills, since you frequently work with others. You must also be creative and able to visualize the future workings of your designs; that is, how they will improve traffic flow, effects on the environment, and potential problems.

EXPLORING

Join a student chapter of the ITE to see if a career in transportation engineering is for you. An application for student membership in the ITE can be obtained by writing the association at the address listed in the For More Information section at the end of this article.

EMPLOYERS

Transportation engineers are employed by federal, state, or local agencies or as private consultants by states, counties, towns, and even neighborhood groups. Many teach or engage in research in colleges and universities.

STARTING OUT

The ITE offers a resume service to students that are members of the organization. Student members can get their resumes published in the *ITE Journal*. The journal also lists available positions for transportation engineering positions throughout the country. Most colleges also offer job placement programs to help transportation engineering graduates locate their first jobs.

ADVANCEMENT

Experienced transportation engineers may advance to become directors of transportation departments or directors of public works in civil service positions. A vast array of related employment in the transportation field is available for those engineers who pursue advanced or continuing education. Transportation engineers may specialize in transportation planning, public transportation (urban and intercity transit), airport engineering, highway engineering, harbor and port engineering, railway engineering, or urban and regional planning.

EARNINGS

Salaries for transportation engineers vary widely depending on duties, qualifications, and experience. According to *U.S. News and World Report*, salaries range from $45,000 to $150,000 a year. The U.S. Department of Labor reports that median annual earnings of civil engineers were $66,190 in 2005. Salaries ranged from less than $44,410 to more than $100,040.

Transportation engineers are also eligible for paid vacation, sick, and personal days, health insurance, pension plans, and in some instances, profit sharing.

WORK ENVIRONMENT

Transportation engineers perform their duties both indoors and out-doors, under a variety of conditions. They are subject to the noise of heavy traffic and various weather conditions while gathering data for some of their studies. They may speak to a wide variety of people as they check the success of their designs. Transportation engineers also spend a fair amount of time in the quiet of an office, making calculations and analyzing the data they have collected in the field. They also spend a considerable amount of time working with computers to optimize traffic signal timing, in general design, and to predict traffic flow.

Transportation engineers must be comfortable working with other professionals, such as transportation technicians, designers, planners, and developers, as they work to create a successful transportation system. At the completion of a project they can take pride in the knowledge that they have made the streets, roads, and highways safer and more efficient as a result of their designs.

OUTLOOK

Employment for civil engineers is expected to increase about as fast as the average for all occupations through 2014, according to the U.S. Department of Labor. More engineers will be needed to work with ITS (Intelligent Transportation System) technology such as electronic toll collection, cameras for traffic incidents/detection, and fiber optics for use in variable message signs. As the population increases and continues to move to suburban areas, qualified transportation engineers will be needed to analyze, assess, and implement traffic plans and designs to ensure safety and the steady, continuous flow of traffic. In cities, transportation engineers will continue to be needed to staff advanced transportation management centers that oversee vast stretches of road using computers, sensors, cameras, and other electrical devices.

FOR MORE INFORMATION

For information regarding fellowships, seminars, and tours, and for general information concerning the transportation engineering field, contact:

American Association of State Highway and Transportation Officials
444 North Capitol Street, NW, Suite 249
Washington, DC 20001-1539
Tel: 202-624-5800
Email: info@aashto.org
http://www.transportation.org

American Public Transportation Association
1666 K Street, NW
Washington, DC 20006-2803
Tel: 202-496-4800
http://www.apta.com

Institute of Transportation Engineers
1099 14th Street, NW, Suite 300 West
Washington, DC 20005-3438
Tel: 202-289-0222
Email: ite_staff@ite.org
http://ww.ite.org

U.S. Department of Transportation
400 Seventh Street, SW
Washington, DC 20590-0001
Tel: 202-366-4000
Email: dot.comments@dot.gov
http://www.dot.gov

Index

A

ABET. *See* Accreditation Board for Engineering and Technology (ABET)
accelerator operators (nuclear engineering) 131
Accreditation Board for Engineering and Technology (ABET) 14, 84, 95, 115
aeronautical and aerospace technicians 60
aeronautical engineers 7
Aerospace America (magazine) 10
aerospace engineers 5–15
  advancement 11–12
  certification/licensing 9
  earnings 12
  employers 10–11
  exploring 9–10
  high school requirements 8
  history 5–6
  job, described 6–8
  outlook 13
  overview 5
  postsecondary training 8–9
  requirements 8–9
  starting out 11
  work environment 12–13
Aerospace Industries Association of America (AIA) 14
Agricola, Georgius 118
AIA (Aerospace Industries Association of America) 14
Aldrin, Edwin "Buzz," Jr. 6
All Engineering Schools (Web site) 70
American Academy of Environmental Engineers 76
American Association of Petroleum Geologists 164
American Association of State Highway and Transportation Officials 196
American Ceramic Society 106
American Chemical Society 28, 31
American Indian Science and Engineering Society 165
American Institute of Aeronautics and Astronautics 14
American Institute of Chemical Engineers 31
American Nuclear Society 135
American Petroleum Institute 165
American Public Transportation Association 196
American Society for Engineering Education (ASEE) 14, 21, 67
American Society for Quality 173

American Society of Certified Engineering Technicians 67
American Society of Civil Engineers 41
American Society of Mechanical Engineers 115–116
American Telephone and Telegraph (AT&T) 44
analytical engineers 7
application engineers 110
applications software engineers 184
Aristotle 23
Armstrong, Neil 6
ASEE. *See* American Society for Engineering Education (ASEE)
ASEE Engineering K12 Center (Web site) 70
ASM International 106
Association for Computing Machinery 84, 189–190
Association for Unmanned Vehicle Systems International 182
ASTM International 173
astronautical engineers 7
AT&T (American Telephone and Telegraph) 44
Avogadro, Amedeo 23–24

B

Baekeland, Leo H. 98
Bell, Alexander Graham 43–44
Bell Telephone Company 44
bioinstrumentation 18
biomaterials 18
biomechanics 18
The Biomedical Engineering Network 22
Biomedical Engineering Society 22
biomedical engineering technicians 60
biomedical engineers 16–22
  advancement 20
  certification/licensing 19
  earnings 20–21
  employers 19–20
  exploring 19
  high school requirements 18
  history 16
  job, described 16–18
  outlook 21
  overview 16
  postsecondary training 19
  requirements 18–19
  starting out 20
  work environment 21

biomedical research 17
Busch, Tom 44–45, 47, 48, 52

C

CAD/CAM engineers 177
Canadian Medical and Biological
  Engineering Society 22
Capek, Karel 174–175
Career Guide: Dun's Employment
  Opportunity Directory 50
Cayley, Sir George 5–6
ceramic design engineers 100
ceramic engineers 99–100
ceramic product sales engineers 100
ceramic research engineers 99–100
ceramic test engineers 100
CFD (computational fluid dynamic) engineers 7
Chemical & Engineering News 74
chemical engineering technicians 61
chemical engineers **23–34**
  advancement 29
  certification/licensing 27
  earnings 30
  employers 28–29
  exploring 28
  high school requirements 26
  history 23–25
  job, described 25–26
  outlook 30–31
  overview 23
  postsecondary training 27
  requirements 26–28
  starting out 29
  Dr. Jennifer Wilcox interview 32–34
  work environment 30
ChemMatters 28
chief engineer (aerospace engineering)
  11
chief engineer (electrical engineering) 50
Christian Brothers University 153
civil engineering technicians 61
civil engineers **35–42**
  advancement 39
  certification/licensing 38
  earnings 40
  employers 39
  exploring 38–39
  high school requirements 38
  history 35–36
  job, described 36–37
  outlook 41
  overview 35
  postsecondary training 38
  requirements 38
  starting out 39
  work environment 40–41
Clemson University 153

computational fluid dynamic (CFD) engineers 7
computer engineers 176
construction engineers 37
consulting engineers 110
Crossroads: The International ACM
  Student Magazine 82

D

Dalton, John 23–24, 127
DeAngelis, Lee 69
The Delphian School 49, 54
De Re Metallica (Agricola) 118
design aerospace engineers 7
design engineer (mechanical engineering)
  109
Devol, George 175
Drake, Edwin 157
drilling engineers 158

E

Edison, Thomas 44
electrical and electronic engineers **43–58,**
  176
  advancement 50–51
  certification/licensing 48
  earnings 51–52
  employers 49
  exploring 49
  high school requirements 47
  history 43–44
  job, described 45–47
  outlook 52–53
  overview 43
  postsecondary training 47–48
  requirements 47–48
  starting out 50
  Timothy D. Swieter interview 54–58
  work environment 52
electrical and electronics engineering technicians 61
Electronic Industries Alliance 53–54
Electronics Technicians Association
  International 68
energy specialists 110
Engineer Girl! (Web site) 70
Engineering, Go For It! (career brochure) 10
engineering manager 158
engineering technicians **59–68**
  certification/licensing 64
  earnings 66
  employers 65
  exploring 65
  high school requirements 63
  history 59
  job, described 59–63
  outlook 67
  overview 59

postsecondary training 63
requirements 63–64
starting out 65–66
work environment 66–67
Environmental Careers Organization 69, 76
environmental engineering technicians 62
environmental engineers **69–77**
advancement 75
certification/licensing 73
earnings 75
employers 74
exploring 74
high school requirements 73
history 69–71
job, described 71–73
outlook 76
overview 69
postsecondary training 73
requirements 73–74
starting out 74
work environment 75–76

F
Faraday, Michael 43
Fermi, Enrico 129
Feynman, Richard 33
fiber optics engineers 138
field engineers 26
field service engineers 46
Ford, Henry 90
Frontiers Program (Worcester Polytechnic Institute) 41

G
Galileo Galilei 136
General Electric Company 44
geological engineers 158
geologists 158
geophysicists 158
Gilbreth, Frank and Lillian 90
Goddard, Robert 6
graphic designers 147

H
Hahn, Otto 127
hardware engineers **78–88**
advancement 83
certification/licensing 80–81
earnings 83
employers 82
exploring 82
high school requirements 80
history 78–79
job, described 79–80
outlook 84

overview 78
postsecondary training 80
requirements 80–81
Reena Singhal interview 85–88
starting out 82–83
work environment 83–84
Hero of Alexandria 174
Huygens, Christiaan 136

I
IEEE. *See* Institute of Electrical and Electronics Engineers (IEEE)
IEEE Computer Society 84, 190
Indiana State University 153
Industrial Engineer (magazine) 92
industrial engineering technicians 62
industrial engineers **89–96,** 176–177
advancement 93–94
certification/licensing 92
earnings 94
employers 93
exploring 92
high school requirements 91
history 89–90
job, described 90–91
outlook 94
overview 89
postsecondary training 91
requirements 91–92
starting out 93
work environment 94
Industrial Revolution 89
Institute for Certification of Computing Professionals 85, 190
Institute of Electrical and Electronics Engineers (IEEE) 53, 85
Institute of Industrial Engineers 95
Institute of Packing Professionals 155
Institute of Transportation Engineers (ITE) 41–42, 196
Institution of Mechanical Engineers 109
International Society of Certified Electronics Technicians 68
International Space Station 6
ITE. *See* Institute of Transportation Engineers (ITE)

J
Jacquard, Joseph-Marie 174
Journal of Petroleum Technology 161
Junior Engineering Technical Society Inc. (JETS) 14, 22, 31, 42, 54, 68, 76, 95, 107, 116, 135, 165

K
Kennedy, John F. 6

L

laser and fiber optics engineers 138
Lasers and Electro-Optics Society 143
Leonardo da Vinci 5, 108

M

Maiman, Theodore H. 136
maintenance and operations engineers 110
manufacturing engineers 110, 177
marketing and sales aerospace engineers 8
Massachusetts Institute of Technology 25
materials aerospace engineers 7
materials engineering technicians 62
materials engineers **97–107**
    advancement 105
    certification/licensing 102–103
    earnings 105
    employers 104
    exploring 103–104
    high school requirements 101
    history 97–99
    job, described 99–101
    outlook 106
    overview 97
    postsecondary training 102
    requirements 101–103
    starting out 104
    work environment 105–106
Maxwell, James C. 136
mechanical engineering technicians 62
mechanical engineers **108–116, 176**
    advancement 114
    certification/licensing 112
    earnings 114
    employers 112–113
    exploring 112
    high school requirements 110–111
    history 108–109
    job, described 109–110
    outlook 115
    overview 108
    postsecondary training 111
    requirements 110–112
    starting out 113–114
    work environment 114–115
metallurgical engineers (metallurgists)
    99
Michigan State University 153
Michigan Technological University 49
Michigan Technological University Summer
    Youth Program 54
The Minerals, Metals & Materials Society
    107, 126
mining engineers **117–126**
    advancement 124
    certification/licensing 122–123
    earnings 124–125
    employers 124
    exploring 123–124
    high school requirements 121–122
    history 117–120
    job, described 120–121
    outlook 125–126
    overview 117
    postsecondary training 122
    requirements 121–123
    starting out 124
    work environment 125
mining equipment engineers 117
Montgolfier, Joseph and Jacques 5
Morse, Samuel 43

N

National Association of Environmental
    Professionals 77
National Engineers Week Headquarters
    31
National Institute of Packaging, Handling,
    and Logistics Engineers 155
National Mining Association 126
National Society of Professional Engineers
    14–15
National Solid Wastes Management
    Association 77
Naval Surface Warfare Center 45
Newcomen, Thomas 108
Newton, Sir Isaac 136
North Carolina State College 129
nuclear criticality safety engineers 130
Nuclear Energy Institute 135
nuclear engineers **127–135**
    advancement 133
    certification/licensing 131–132
    earnings 133–134
    employers 132–133
    exploring 132
    high school requirements 131
    history 127–129
    job, described 129–131
    outlook 134–135
    overview 127
    postsecondary training 131
    requirements 131–132
    starting out 133
    work environment 134
nuclear fuels reclamation engineers 130–
    131
nuclear fuels research engineers 130–
    131
nuclear health physicists 130

O

oil-well equipment and services sales engi-
    neer 159
oil-well equipment research engineer
    159

oil-well equipment test engineer 159
optical engineers **136–144**
    advancement 141–142
    certification/licensing 140
    earnings 142
    employers 141
    exploring 140–141
    high school requirements 139
    history 136–137
    job, described 137–138
    outlook 143
    overview 136
    postsecondary training 139–140
    requirements 139–140
    starting out 141
    work environment 142–143
Optical Society of America 143
Optics Education (Web site) 144
Optics for Teens (Web site) 144
Optics Report 142
Otto, Nicolaus 109

P
packaging designers 147
Packaging Digest 150
packaging engineers **145–155**
    advancement 151–152
    certification/licensing 149–150
    earnings 152
    employers 150–151
    exploring 150
    high school requirements 148
    history 145–146
    job, described 146–148
    outlook 154–155
    overview 145
    postsecondary training 148–149
    requirements 148–150
    starting out 151
    work environment 154
Packaging Machinery Manufacturers
    Institute 155
Packaging World 150
Paris, Bonnie 95–96
petroleum engineering technicians 62
petroleum engineers **156–165**
    advancement 162
    certification/licensing 160
    earnings 162–163
    employers 161
    exploring 160–161
    high school requirements 159
    history 156–157
    job, described 157–159
    outlook 164
    overview 156
    postsecondary training 159–160
    requirements 159–160

    starting out 161–162
    work environment 163–164
pipeline engineers 37
plastics applications engineers 101
plastics engineers 100–101
plastics process engineers 101
plastics research specialists 101
Pollution Engineering (journal) 74
Pre-Engineering Times 49, 92
Prior, Calvin 79–80
process design engineers 26
process engineers 110
production engineers 26, 46, 158–159
professors 46–47
project engineers 26
project team leaders 187

Q
quality control engineers **166–173**
    advancement 171
    certification/licensing 169–170
    earnings 171
    employers 170
    exploring 170
    high school requirements 169
    history 166–168
    job, described 168–169
    outlook 172–173
    overview 166
    postsecondary training 169
    requirements 169–170
    starting out 171
    work environment 171–172

R
radiation protection technicians 130
rehabilitation engineering 18
research chief engineer 159
research engineers 25, 109
reservoir engineers 158
The Robotics Alliance Project 182
Robotics and Automation Society 182
robotics engineers **174–182**
    advancement 179–180
    earnings 180
    employers 179
    exploring 178–179
    high school requirements 177
    history 174–175
    job, described 175–177
    outlook 181–182
    overview 174
    postsecondary training 177–178
    requirements 177–178
    starting out 179
    work environment 180–181
Robotics Industries Association 182
robotics technicians 62

Rochester Institute of Technology 153
R.U.R. (Capek) 174–175

S

safety engineers 117
sales engineers 110
SCA (Student Conservation Association)
77
scanners (nuclear engineering) 131
School of Military Packaging Technology
155
A Sightseer's Guide to Engineering (Web
site) 70
Singhal, Reena 85–88
*Six Easy Pieces: Essentials of Physics
Explained by Its Most Brilliant Teacher*
(Feynman) 33
Six Sigma 167–168
Sloan Career Cornerstone Center 85
Society for Mining, Metallurgy, and
Exploration 107, 126
Society of Manufacturing Engineers (SME)
32, 116, 182
Society of Petroleum Engineers 165
Society of Plastics Engineers (SPE) 107
Society of Women Engineers 32, 135
software engineering technicians 185
software engineers **183–190**
advancement 187–188
certification/licensing 186
earnings 188
employers 187
exploring 187
high school requirements 186
history 183
job, described 184–186
outlook 189
overview 183
postsecondary training 186
requirements 186
starting out 187
work environment 188–189
Software & Information Industry
Association 190
software managers 188
SPE (Society of Plastics Engineers) 107
SPIE--The International Society for Optical
Engineering 144
Sputnik I 6
Strassman, Fritz 127
structural engineers. *See* civil engineers
Student Conservation Association (SCA)
77
surveying and mapping engineers 37
Swieter, Timothy D. 54–58

systems physiology (biomedical engineering) 18
systems software engineers 184

T

Taylor, Frederick 90
technical sales engineers 26
Tesla, Nicholas 44
testing engineers 109–110
Total Quality Management (TQM)
167–168
transportation engineers 37, **191–196**
advancement 194–195
certification/licensing 193–194
earnings 195
employers 194
exploring 194
high school requirements 193
history 191
job, described 192–193
outlook 195–196
overview 191
postsecondary training 193
requirements 193–194
starting out 194
work environment 195
transportation technicians 192

U

Unimation (Universal Automation) 175
University of Florida 153
University of Illinois--Urbana-Champagne
153
University of North Dakota 15
University of Wisconsin--Stout 153
U.S. Department of Energy 135
U.S. Department of Transportation 196

V

Volta, Alexander 43

W

Watt, James 109
Waxman, Mike 70–71
Wilcox, Jennifer 32–34
Worcester Polytechnic Institute 165
Worcester Polytechnic Institute Frontiers
Program 41
Work in Optics (Web site) 144
Wright, Orville 6
Wright, Wilbur 6

Y

Yahoo: Engineering (Web site) 70